Caboose Anatomy

The caboose is the operating headquarters and office of the freight train. At his table-desk, the conductor spends as much as half his time on paper work which includes handling the waybills and the wheel report listing in detail the cars of his train with owners' initials and numbers, together with contents and weight. One or two brakemen also ride the caboose, taking care of such routine as switching, flagging and watching the train for hot boxes. The brakeman on the rear platform signals to a passing train that all is in order. The brakeman in the cupola keeps a sharp lookout to spot any trouble that might show up on the train ahead. He also watches for signals from the head-end brakeman or the engine crew, and they talk to each other by radio-telephone. In the lockers, mostly below the cupola, the trainmen store their food which can be cooked on the pot-bellied stove to furnish amply satisfying meals or a hot cup of coffee.—NEW YORK CENTRAL

Tradition has it that the friendly conductor is the head of the train. The freight conductor's uniform consists of bib-overalls and an ordinary hat. On the front of his hat the word *CONDUCTOR* blazoned in metal indicates his office.—DONALD DUKE

THE
RAILROAD
CABOOSE

Its 100 Year History, Legend and Lore

by WILLIAM F. KNAPKE
with FREEMAN HUBBARD

Golden West Books
San Marino, California

THE RAILROAD CABOOSE

Copyright © 1968 by Freeman Hubbard

Golden West Books

A Division of Pacific Railroad Publications, Inc.

P.O. BOX 8136 • SAN MARINO, CALIFORNIA • 91108

Table Of Contents

The caboose is the punctuation mark that concludes every freight train, it's the trainmen's living room, his office, workshop, kitchen, dining room, bedroom, den and toilet. Here a modern day Chicago & North Western bay window caboose clatters across the Namekagon River near Trego, Wisconsin.—PHIL HASTINGS

Foreword

W HAT IS a caboose? Formally, it's the punctuation mark that concludes every freight train . . . a mobile office . . . a lookout post. It's also the most vulnerable victim of the ugly, often terrifying backlash of slack action. Or the only shelter when the flanger gets on the ground and snow closes in the line ahead and behind. Or a coffin if the second section overruns your flagman in fog. A caboose is a van on the Canadian National, a cabin car on the Pennsylvania, a buggy on the Boston & Maine, a cab on Chesapeake & Ohio; but by whatever name, the caboose remains as symbolic a fixture of the American railroad scene as exists. For whereas steam and semaphores have virtually vanished, and the *Official Guide* has lost its last heavyweight 12-Section, one-drawing-room Pullman of traditional configuration, and the names Nashville, Chattanooga & St. Louis and Nickel Plate are no more, the caboose with a cupola rides on in what historians deem to be at least its 110th year. In 1966, 14,886 cabooses were in the employ of class one U.S. railroads, and the newest complement in modernity the diesels at the other end of their trains, for they include roller bearings, electric lighting, radiophones, even seat belts.

Little red caboose ... oh, what memories that childhood storybook phrase evokes for any man fortunate enough to have watched and heard the miles recede behind the markers of one! One of my most powerful, indelible memories is of a summer evening on the Cotton Belt which I spent in the cupola of a caboose tied to a 4-8-4 and 2,000 tons of perishables. Lightning played tag across the sky as we bounded over momentum grades en route from Tyler to Texarkana, then darkness and thunder and rain closed in upon us. The description in *Trains* reads like this: "Thunder mixes with yellow flashes of lightning over Texas ... The tiny glow of the cab light bulb in the Northern, 44 cars forward, comes back through the black of a rainy evening—and periodically the electrical storm lights up the entire weaving, rocking consist for a brief, vivid portrait of a redball schedule heading home."

There—that hints at what a first-row seat to railroading a caboose can be. But, at least in the limited reference of my experience, a caboose is synonymous with much, much more. It can wham the guts out of you descending the eastern slope of the Sierra with tonnage on the Southern Pacific. It embraces the sweet smell of honeysuckle and overlooks the green of young tobacco plants on a mixed train on the Louisville & Nashville. On a caboose you hear the engineer's parentage discussed, not to mention the trainmaster's, and on a caboose you can drink the best coffee and attempt to swallow the worst.

And as you'll discover in this book, caboose architecture was and is as imaginative as the mold of steam itself. Side-door, cupola, bay-window, four-wheel, streamlined—the caboose has sampled all. As a boy I delighted in Pennsy's vest pocket, two-axle cabooses (pardon me, "cabin cars"), not to mention the rifle-slot vision of central cupolas compressed by tight clearances. L&N used to own the all-American caboose in my estimation—bright red outside, apple green inside, centered cupola, black leather cushions—and then it built the ugliest great cumbersome boxcars of crummies.

Oh yes. Indulge me, please, in another item of caboose lore. What is more graceful than a conductor catching the rear step of a caboose moving past the yard office at, say, 10 to 15 m.p.h.? Nothing, absolutely nothing.

But let Bill Knapke tell us about cabooses, for he is the professional. An authentic boomer and a born storyteller, Bill has spent a lifetime riding cabooses for pay. In this volume he fills a vacant notch on the shelf of anyone's railroad library. I recommend both him and his subject to you in the warmest possible terms.

David P. Morgan

July 1967
Editor—*Trains* Magazine
Milwaukee, Wisconsin

Remember the night of the big sleet, oldtimer? Heat from the caboose stove glowed and darkened in pulsing waves from the cherry red fire, and the red and white lantern reflections danced about the steel top counter. On the wall hung the familiar tin coffee cup and on the round-bellied stove a steaming kettle. This was railroading!—PHIL HASTINGS

ONE

Little Red Caboose Behind The Train

O, the brake-wheel's old and rusty, the shoes are thin and worn,
   And she's loaded down with link and pin and chain,
And there's danger all around us as we try to pound our ear
   In the little red caboose behind the train.
                                         —from an old folksong

REMEMBER the night of a big sleet, oldtimer? Violent winds were rattling the cupola windows of a Southern Pacific caboose, threatening to blow them in, and you heard, muted by storm and train sounds, *Wha-a-a-a, wha-a, wha-a, wha-a,*—the long and three short blasts of a locomotive whistle that bade you go out into the howling darkness and walk back the variable "required distance" to protect the rear of your train. You glanced at the air gauge.

"Nope, not a busted air hose," you muttered. "Hell's bells, it'd hafta be a night like this for something to go wrong."

The conductor grinned sympathy. Lifting the lid of the round-bellied stove, he peered down at the dancing flames but said nothing. You slid into your heavy coat, turned up the collar, and pulled on your cap and gloves. Then you grabbed red and white lanterns and two fuses. Outside, you waited on the icy steps. When

11

the speed slackened, you unloaded and fought the windy sleet as you walked, counting your steps.

Will you ever forget the biting cold of that next hour? You stomped on the crisp slippery right-of-way and threshed your arms about to keep from freezing. The long wait seemed like eternity. At length, when you felt you couldn't hold out any longer, you heard the rapturous music of four long blasts of an engine whistling in the flag. It came faintly through the tempest but you could have heard it even if it hadn't been half so loud.

You twisted the bonnet off a fusee, cracked it to emit a fiery pink glare, jabbed it into a sleet-encrusted tie end, and battled your way back to the warmth of civilization, hoping the conductor hadn't let the fire get too low. He hadn't. Actually, the friendly stove was almost white-hot, and the Old Man insisted on helping you off with your stiff glistening coat and gloves. He told you to lie down near the stove, which you did. You listened to the muffled drone of wheels rolling beneath you and you thought, is there any spot on earth more comfortable?

Such incidents explain the trainman's affection for his caboose in the days when practically every one had a cupola, often called the doghouse or sun parlor. No wonder he loved this car. It sheltered him from winter storms and summer heat. Here, to the tune of wheels clicking over rail joints, he worked and argued, cooked and ate his meals, played, relaxed, and slept. I have known very few oldtime trainmen who did not feel sentimental about this form of equipment.

"My fond recollection of cabooses," G. H. Harris, past president of the Order of Railway Conductors and Brakemen, told me, "dates from the years when I rode and lived in them during and shortly after World War II. As will be recalled by many of us who were in road service then, the time spent at home was seldom and it could not be anticipated with regularity. To such men our caboose was not only a 'home away from home' but also, all too frequently, a place in which we lived for greater periods than we did at our legal residences.

"I was fortunate in having a good caboose assigned to me in the early 1940's. Rebuilt from the stripped-down framework of an old 36-foot Baltimore & Ohio car, it had bay windows and a custom-

Trainmen never forget the biting cold of winter. They stomp the crisp slippery right-of-way and thresh their arms to keep from freezing. At last the rapturous music of four long blasts from the steam locomotive whistle calling in the flag. The conductor twists the bonnet off the fusee and waves a *Highball.*—PHIL HASTINGS

built icebox, the latter by courtesy of a friendly car foreman. My regular brakeman and I further equipped it into what was truly—for the era we were railroading in—a rolling home on wheels.

"Kerosene lights were not good enough for us then. We managed to wire the car for electricity with a long extension cord that enabled us to plug into the nearest 110-volt circuit at each caboose track we were parked on at a terminal or away-from-home point of a regular run. In turn, for summer time, this gave us an electric fan for cooling purposes and electric hot-plates for cooking, and radios, and other little luxury items. We also managed to have on board a small gasoline stove (even though it was not strictly according to regulations) so that between terminals we could prepare coffee and even full meals when we were lying in sidetracks or at points where our caboose was not readily parked near a handy electrical outlet."

The caboose was the original house trailer. It included the trainman's living room, his office, workshop, kitchen, dining room, bedroom, den, toilet, balcony, and observation tower. It was his source of income and personal prestige. Also his means of travel. Join a railroad crew and see the world! How many a wide-eyed farm boy and bored factory hand answered that call in simpler or easier yesterdays! The caboose was a daily adventure that took you far from your native city or town—a window on the world. Naturally, you became attached to it.

For well over a century this multi-purpose vehicle has played a vital role in freight shipment. On millions of runs it has tagged along behind merchandise hotshots and peddler locals, work extras, and supply trains. It tails loads of copper in my home state of Arizona, iron ore from the Mesabi Range, Saskatchewan wheat, Texas livestock, citrus fruit from California and Florida, granite from Vermont, and "Paul Bunyan's toothpicks" from the big woods.

Just about every freight train on our continent has a caboose. Among the relatively few exceptions are the single-track Jackass & Western Railroad trains that are run by remote control from the nuclear research laboratory at Jackass Flats in the Arizona desert. Also the world's first crewless freight trains, that wheel iron ore on the single-track Quebec, North Shore & Labrador line 24 hours a day, seven days a week throughout the year, in a bleak wilderness 850 miles from the Arctic Circle.

Most circus trains for the past century have had cabooses. I remember when Ringling Brothers and Barnum & Bailey operated the biggest circus of all time, throughout the United States and Canada. There were 100 cars, all told. "The Greatest Show on Earth" owned every one of them and operated them all simultaneously in a train of four sections, with a caboose on the tail of each section. The Number One circus was very important then. Among other attractions, it boasted a herd of 55 elephants—more than Hannibal's army took across the Alps to invade Rome over two thousand years ago!

One day a playful elephant on this circus train extended her long trunk out of her oversized car and picked up a "flimsy" that had been placed on a train-order stand beside the Milwaukee Road track for the conductor riding the caboose. Luckily, the telegraph operator, standing outside his office, had seen the trick. Rushing back inside, he snatched a duplicate copy of the order off a hook and managed to insert it into the arm of the wayside installation before the waycar of the slow-moving "caravan of dreams" rumbled by.

Some silk trains had cabooses but most of them hadn't. If your crummy was latched onto a silk special you had something to brag about. Those trains really traveled. The Southern Pacific had plenty of them. So did the Union Pacific, Great Northern, Santa Fe, Northern Pacific, Canadian Pacific and Canadian National, Milwaukee Road, and several Eastern roads.

Silk cargoes, often worth millions, were landed at West Coast ports from fast ocean liners, were loaded into reefers and express cars, and were highballed to Eastern markets at full speed. It was a race against high insurance costs, fluctuating silk prices, spoilage (shipments usually consisted of live silkworms in cocoons packed in bales), and possible hijacking, for the Al Capone gang and its ilk flourished in the latter part of that era. Those trains were given rights over everything. Even the lordly *Overland Limited*, the Union Pacific's pride, on which passengers paid $10 extra fare, had to go "in the hole" for silk. There was very little sleeping in cabooses on those runs. Even when you had a spot of free time, the

waycar bounced so much that it was next to impossible for you to "grab shut-eye." But cabooses were not often used in highballing silk because of their light weight and insufficient ballast.

For a different reason the most popular of all consists, the pay-train ("money-wagon") generally ran without a caboose. That was because the train crew, the paymaster, his assistant, and the armed guards often rode in the pay-car itself and had their meals prepared in it by a professional cook. In some cases, though, especially when the money-wagon was small or needed extra guards, a caboose was coupled behind to serve as kitchen, dining room, and sleeping quarters.

How well I recall those days long ago when many railroads paid their workers in gold, silver, and small currency! Today no pay-train is left in North America, except on the National Railways of Mexico, which now pays by check so that this train does not need armed guards or a caboose. Incidentally, the Canadian Pacific's

A caboose hop (engine and way car) on the old Hocking Valley Line.

second pay-car, No. 137, built in 1882 at the Brockville & Ontario Railway shops in Perth, Ontario, was converted in 1886 to a conductor's van (caboose).

During America's pay-car era, redball freights clipping off the miles at passenger-train speed were few and far between—if, indeed, there were any at all, aside from the silk specials. Lesser freights jogged along with innumerable stops for set-outs and pickups, not to mention delays from hotboxes (overheated journals), defective track, and other mechanical difficulties. It was not uncommon, after human endurance had just about reached the limit, for your train to "tie up" at some sleeping village that seemed like a thousand miles from the nearest "greasy spoon" or flophouse. Most of the cabooses I knew were fully equipped for such emergencies.

The much-scarred waycar desks on which skippers made out their reports were used also for writing personal letters and even

17

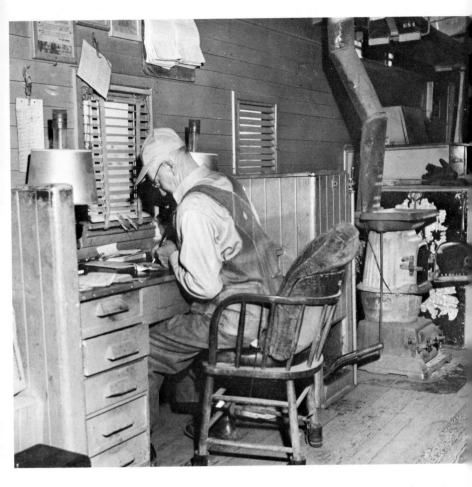

Southern Pacific conductor Charles Martin records trip report in the train office. The conductor's train book was often called the *First Reader* in old time railroad lingo.—STAN KISTLER

in rare instances, verse and magazine stories. There has been a heap of living in cabooses. Many a conductor became so fond of his work headquarters that, when he retired, he bought it for a song, had it shipped to his home and set up in his back yard, and subsequently spent many happy hours within its familiar walls. At least one couple, to my knowledge, were legitimately married in a caboose and I have seen authenticated records of babies born in such vehicles.

Yes, this piece of equipment has had a romantic history in more ways than one. Many cabooses have carried passengers, particularly those on branch lines and short railroads, and a very few still do. Others have accommodated animal mascots and birds. Men have been hired and fired in cabooses. There used to be a time when a conductor could pick up a farm hand at one of his stops and put him on the company payroll as a brakeman, but that was long, long ago. Nobody knows how many cabooses have been involved in runaways, freak accidents, and fatal wrecks. Dig deep enough into caboose lore and you'll come up with almost anything, even murder and suicide. But such doings are never mentioned in the company's annual report to its stockholders.

Like the old gray mare, this little car "ain't what she usta be." No longer does a seasoned conductor regard it as his personal property. Instead of being assigned to one man on a more or less permanent basis, it is more likely to be pooled. Modern crew men cannot store their belongings in a waycar nor put provisions in its cupboard with the assurance that they will work, eat, and sleep in the same vehicle on their next run.

At this writing, the Western Pacific, like many other roads, has just signed an agreement with the Order of Railway Conductors and Brakemen preserving the extra pay allowance which it granted some time ago to conductors and trainmen in through freight service where cabooses have been pooled. G. H. Harris, who played a leading role in such parleys, informed me:

"Truly an era is passing as more and more of our Order's representatives agree in negotiations with the carriers to replace the old assigned cabooses with pooled ones. Most of the latter are either newly rebuilt or recently remodeled. They include such luxuries as electric refrigerators, flush toilets, generators or alter-

Trainman Robert Selanders of Southern Pacific extra 6311 East hoops up a "19 order" as the freight whips through Cape Horn, California.
—PHIL HASTINGS

Hooping up train orders as a fast extra freight rolls through Saugus, California, on the Southern Pacific. —RICHARD STEINHEIMER *(Below)* Canadian National freight conductors hand notes to one another as their trains pass near Edmunston, New Brunswick. —PHIL HASTINGS

nators for electric power for marker and interior lights, and two-way radio equipment. Many even have safety seat-belts for crew men occupying seats in bay windows or cupolas, because of the greater amount of slack in modern times, brought about by the extended length of freight trains.

"Progress, of course, cannot be stopped. The changing caboose is only one aspect of the revolution taking place everywhere. We live in a computer age that relegates to the past the glorious era when railroading's pace was more leisurely and the conductors and brakemen were more closely knit through their 'palace on wheels.' "

Before going further into these changes, let's turn to the origin and development of the North American caboose, what it looked like inside, and how it compared with its European counterparts.

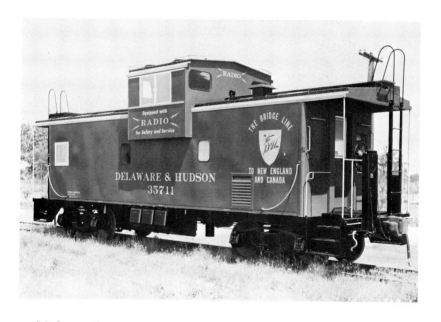

Modern radio equipped way car on the Delaware & Hudson has a saddlebag type cupola. *(Left)* On the Denver & Rio Grande Western narrow gauge line running between Durango and Alamosa, a colorful reddish caboose concludes a string of tanks from a Chama refinery.— DONALD DUKE

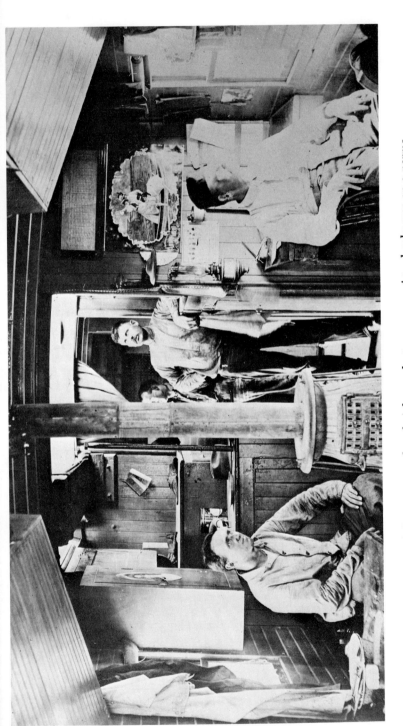

At the turn of the century, when freight conductors were assigned cabooses on a permanent basis and when train crews lived in them for days at a time, this shot was made on the Southern Pacific's Tucson Division. Picture on the rear wall shows the typical pin-up girl of the period, wearing long skirt, in a row boat.—SOUTHERN PACIFIC

TWO

How It Originated

C ABOOSE was originally a nautical term. Its first definition in *Webster's New International Dictionary* is "a house on deck where the cooking is done; a galley." Second is the common railroad meaning and third is "an open-air cooking oven." Various wordbooks liken it to the English *cabin*, the Dutch *kabuis* and *kombuis*, the Danish *kabys*, the Swedish *kabysa*, the Low German *kabuus*, and German *kabuse*, each meaning "a little room or hut." According to *The American Collegiate Dictionary*, the caboose in the United States is "a car (usually the last) on a freight train, used by the train crew" and in Great Britain "a kitchen on the deck of a ship; a galley."

From the very first, the preparation and eating of meals on railroad cabooses was standard practice—and still is, to a lesser extent. Besides being the conductor's cabin and the galley, the waycar in its heyday was the fo'csle and the crow's nest, or lookout. One famous caboose on the Erie Railroad reverted to type, so to speak, by actually going to sea as part of a ship's equipment; a later chapter will tell you about it. Perhaps because Cornelius Vanderbilt made a fortune in the steamship business and acquired the title of Commodore before he founded the New

The Canadian Pacific term for caboose, as seen here, is *Conductor's Van.*

York Central, he may have had something to do with introducing the marine word into railroad usage.

The caboose has had more names than any other piece of railroad equipment, even more than the locomotive. Some are technical terms, some sentimental, and others derogatory. Among the best-known ones are waycar, cabin, cab and conductor's car. In Canada and Britain the word is van or brake-van.

At the height of the boomer era, when countless railroad men in all branches of service roamed North America from one job to another, sometimes from one division to another on the same road, considerable rail slang was in vogue. The terminology varied on different roads and in geographical areas, although the boomers rambled so much that their lingo was pretty well understood wherever trains ran in English-speaking North America. Most of this lingo has since passed out of common usage, but oldtimers still use colorful remnants of it now and then.

Among the picturesque terms that boomers coined to describe the caboose are ambulance, anchor, buggy, brain-box (the conductor was often called "the brains"), bazoo wagon, chariot (this word more often designated an official's private car, technically a business car), crummy (very common), cripples' home, den, diner, glory wagon (men killed in train wrecks, caboose or otherwise, "went to glory"), go-cart, hack (very common), kitchen, madhouse, monkey cage or monkey hut (also many other kinds of cages, mostly derogatory), palace, parlor (rear brakeman was "parlor brakeman" or "parlor shack"), perambulator, rest room, treasure chest, and zoo—plus some terms that are not printable.

The first caboose on record was rather primitive, being merely the last boxcar of a mixed (passenger-freight) train on the old Auburn & Syracuse, a 26-mile line later absorbed by the New York Central. From this car in the 1840's conductor Nat Williams ran his train. In it he kept flags, lanterns, chains, tools, etc., and wrote his reports while seated on a wooden box, using an up-ended barrel as a desk, and ate his meals on the same barrel-top out of a lunch pail brought from home.

In effect, Nat's car was a caboose. The first known use of this word, in 1885, referred to conductors' cars on the Buffalo, Corning & New York line, now part of the Erie-Lackawanna system. Four years later, according to *The New York Times*, a trainman named Edgerton sued Commodore Vanderbilt's New York & Harlem Railway (a predecessor of the New York Central) for injuries he received February 29, 1859, in a "caboose car." No further details of the case are available.

Meanwhile, in January 1851, Erie Railroad passengers who had occasion to travel through Suffern, New York, were amused and mystified by something new at Mountain Switch, just west of the Mountain House. Set out on the ground near the track was an ordinary, small, wooden boxcar such as those which served in those days as living quarters for trainmen. It was only 25 feet long but very wide, as the Erie's track gauge was then six feet, and its trucks had been removed.

But this boxcar was unlike all others in two respects. Many telegraph wires connected it with the regular pole line that paralleled the rails through Suffern. Also, an extra half-story had been built out of the roof of the original car, and windows had been cut into all four sides of the little observatory. Thus the car's occupants, by climbing a short wooden ladder to a platform erected inside the car and about three feet lower than the main roof, could see some distance in all directions.

The workmen who occupied this unique setup had been sent to Suffern by Charles Minot, the Erie's superintendent, to install tape telegraph instruments and the electric batteries used in those days. Their leader was Dave Hen Conklin, first telegraph operator on the Erie (salary $30 per month). His regular job also included stringing wires, making repairs after storms, and locating open wires or grounds. He was a busy man, a smart electrician, and his crew turned in a good performance at Suffern.

For some time this car, with its network of clinging wires and glass insulators, its tiny telegraph pole, and its cupola set at one end of the roof, stood beside the rails at Mountain Switch. With its assignment finished, it was put on trucks again and sent on a winding 17-mile journey through the wooded Rockland Hills to the Erie's Piermont Shops to be converted into a standard conductor's car—*i.e.*, a boxcar equipped with a stove, lamps, and two or three bunks but no cupola. At this point history is obscure. The claim has been made that the unique car started a trend on the Erie for cabin cars with cupolas, but no record is available to prove it. All we know for certain is that the Erie had one cupola car, not a caboose, as early as 1851. The Erie genius, possibly the inventive Charles Minot who devised the car cupola, may have given further thought to the subject and eventually applied it to the cabin car also.

Some of the earliest cabooses were flatcars on which shanties or cabins were built (a few roads still refer to their cabooses as cabin cars), but most of them were boxcars with windows and side doors, equipped with facilities for working, eating, and sleeping. Many such cars doubled as baggage cars. Others regularly carried passengers and were listed as accommodation cars—a practice which has never completely died out. Early in 1966 the West Virginia Public Service Commission heard testimony that, in an effort to "make a case" for discontinuance of certain passenger trains, the Baltimore & Ohio had taken the coaches off, required passengers to ride in a caboose, changed departure and arrival times to inconvenient hours, and refused to sell tickets, thus discouraging patronage. At this writing, however, although passengers continue to ride the caboose, the trains are still in service. Furthermore, on some tourist-attraction shortlines operated by steam power an added appeal is to ride in an old-style waycar. Years ago, certain railroads and branches which did not have ordinary passenger

service carried travelers, usually but not always for pay, in cabooses at the end of freight trains. The following poem memorializ-
ing this practice was written by Maude K. Backlund:

Perched on a high spring wagon-seat,
  I have driven to town with a load of wheat,
On a hayrack heaped with coarse slough hay;
  Over the rangeland, far and wide
On a tricky bronch the herd I'd ride.

But I rode to the county seat in state
  In the red caboose of the local freight
And watched the track slip out and away,
  With the telegraph poles, across the plain;
Prairie and track and the moving train

All that a searching human eye
  Could see in the circle beneath the sky.
I may travel long and may travel far
  In liner or clipper or palace car,
But never so long that I could forget

Coming in from the dark and wet
  To the shelter and warmth of the rough clean shack
At the end of a freight on the track;
  Never so far that my dream turned loose
Would not carry me back to the old caboose.

The most widely accepted version of the origin of the caboose
cupola gives the credit to T. B. Watson, a Chicago & North
Western freight conductor running between Cedar Rapids and
Clinton, Iowa. One bright summer day in 1863, about the time the
Battle of Gettysburg was being fought in Pennsylvania, Watson's
flat-topped caboose was assigned temporarily to a work-train and
he used an old boxcar instead. According to the story, this car had
a large hole in the roof and the whimsical Watson piled boxes on
the floor and sat atop one in such a way that his head and
shoulders protruded above the roof. This odd position gave him a
fine view of his train and the Iowa prairie. It is likely that he
watched cattle grazing, farmers mowing hay, and gophers scurry-
ing into their holes and, while passing through villages, waved at

29

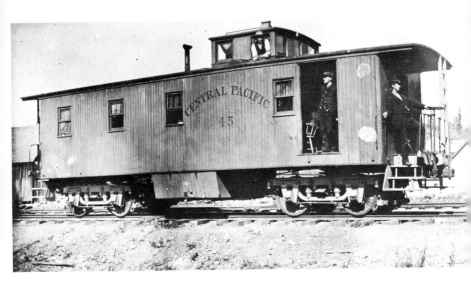

Wood body, coal stove, cupola, and kerosene lamp were standard in all oldtime Central Pacific (now Southern Pacific) crummies where train crews lived for days at a time. In the view above, caboose No. 45, built in August 1872, with wood frame trucks and crew capacity of 10. *(Below)* This 1885 vintage caboose cost the Central Pacific $838 to build and carried the latest design Arch-Bar leaf spring caboose trucks.—BOTH GERALD M. BEST COLLECTION

girls from his lofty perch. In any event, it must have been a pleasant ride.

Watson decided, so the story goes, that if all cabooses had cupolas the trainmen's work would be easier. Upon arrival at Clinton, he sought out the master mechanic, told him about the trip, and suggested that "crow's nests" be included in the two new waycars then being built at the North Western shops there. The official agreed, the cars were constructed that way, and thus the C&NW may have been the first railroad to operate cabooses with cupolas.

But for the next few years the use of such equipment was purely local. America's railroads have taken slowly to new ideas. In fact, in 1869, when the iron rails were joined at Promontory, Utah, for the nation's first transcontinental line, neither of the two roads involved—the Union Pacific and the Central Pacific (now Southern Pacific)—had a cupolaed caboose. Four years later, the first edition of *Master Car Builder's Dictionary* listed the word *caboose* but did not mention cupola. But the second edition, in 1884, stated: "Cabooses are often made with lookouts for displaying train signals to locomotives and following trains, and to give trainmen a view of the train."

There is no record of when the cupola first became popular, but the caboose lore in song and story refers mainly to cars with this improvement. Today, many of the most modern cabooses, like the earliest ones, do not have cupolas. As a rule, big roads no longer need the "sun parlor," which was devised for visibility over the car tops, for accessibility to hand-brakes, and for greater ease in signaling to the engineer. An increasing number of conductors, while breezing over the road, keep in touch with the head end by short-wave radio-telephone. Air-brakes have replaced hand-brakes, and plenty of trains today are more than a mile long. With a giant-size boxcar just ahead of a little crummy, your visibility would be like facing a tight board fence; but even if there were no jumbos, how many trainmen seated in the doghouse could make out the details of what's happening to cars a mile or so up ahead? But oldtimers like myself regret the passing, on so many roads, of the time-honored cupola.

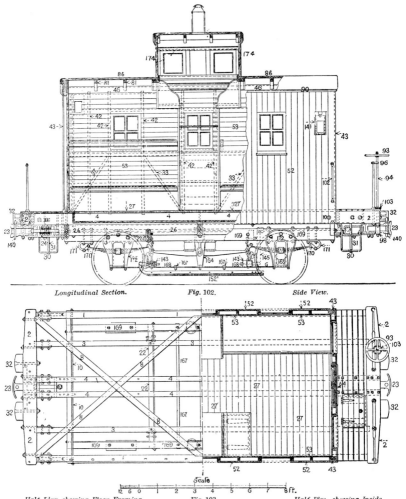

Longitudinal Section.   *Fig.* 102.   *Side View.*

Half Plan, showing Floor Framing.   *Fig.* 103.   *Half Plan., showing Inside*

FOUR-WHEELED CABOOSE CAR, *with* LOOKOUT, PENNSYLVANIA RAILROAD AND ALLIED LINES.
(Old style. The present standard, modified from the above, is shown in Figs. 45-6-7.)

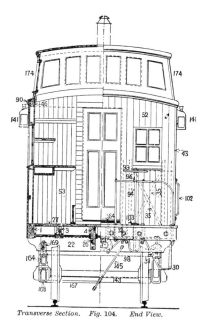

NAMES OF PARTS; *Figs.* 102–104.

1. *Side-sill.*
2. *End-sill.*
3. *Intermediate-sill.*
4. *Centre-sill.*
5. *Short Floor-timber.*
6. *Brake-hanger Timber.*
8. *Floor-timber Braces.*
10. *Sill Tie rod.*
22. *Needle-beam* or *Cross-frame Tie-timber.*
23. *Drawbar.*
24. *Draw-spring.*
26. *Draw timbers.*
27. *Floor.*
30. *Sill-step.*
31. *Sill-step Stay.*
32. *Dead-blocks.*
33. *Side Body-brace.*
35. *End Body-brace.*
37. *Body-counterbrace.*
42. *Body post.*
43. *Corner-post.*
46. *Plate.*
52. *Sheathing* or *Siding.*
53. *Inside-lining.*
64. *Door-sill.*
81. *Carline* or *Carling.*
86. *Roof-boards.*
90. *Eaves-moulding.*
93. *Brake-wheel.*
94. *Brake-shaft.*
96. *Upper Brake-shaft Bearing.*
98. *Brake-shaft Step.*
102. *Corner Grab-iron.*
103. *Brake Ratchet-wheel.*
140. *Coupling-pin.*
141. *Train Signal-lamp.*
143. *Brake-beam.*
145. *Brake-lever.*
152'. *Lower Brake-rod.*
165. *Journal-box.*
167. *Pedestal Stay-rod.*
168. *Pedestal Tie-bar.*
169. *Pedestal-timber.*
170. *Spring-hanger.*
171. *Spring-hanger Iron.*
172. *Pedestal.*
174. *Lookout.*

(Parts numbered 8, 164, 170, 171 and 174 are special to this car, and appear nowhere else.)

Transverse Section. Fig. 104. *End View.*

Fig. 104½. *Perspective View.*
FOUR-WHEELED CABOOSE CAR, PENNSYLVANIA RAILROAD.
(*Old style; for new, see Figs. 45–47.*)

The railroad caboose with lookout as it first appeared in the 1888 edition of the *Car-Builders Dictionary,* compiled for the Master Car-Builders' Association—GERALD M. BEST COLLECTION

The caboose was, and is, basically the working headquarters of the freight conductor and his rear brakeman. Before the advent of the bay-window or traveling-office type, all cabooses looked somewhat alike inside. Of course, the arrangement of closets, stove, desk, bunks, and sun parlor varied, but the essentials were there. Upon entering the front door you found a locker on each side—really long boxes with hinged lids—usually extending from one end of the car to the cupola wall. Some cabooses omitted a section or one or both lockers to make space for a desk or a coalbox. The heavy cast-iron stove, generally without legs, was bolted to the wall. Here and there, almost within arm's reach, the wall was cluttered with pigeon-holes, racks, and occasionally cigar-boxes minus one end, stuffed with papers. A kerosene lamp secured by brackets to prevent its being upset shed light when necessary.

Cupola placement showed much diversity. You might find it almost anywhere from an extreme end of the car to the exact middle, as the designer wished. I could never see any advantage to one spot over another, the function in each case being the same. Throughout the caboose were closets and cupboards galore, mostly built into, under, or around the cupola base. They provided storage space for cooking utensils, food, clothing, and so on. The long lockers, covered with equally long flat cushions or pads, served only as seats and cots but not to hold journal brasses, knuckles, knuckle pins, and other hardware. Under the body of most way-cars was an additional locker known as a "possum belly" in which we kept a jack, wrecking chains, and "dope" (oil and waste for cooling overheated journals).

Before freight trains had air-brakes, unused locker space was generally filled with short pieces of rail, scrap iron, and other heavy material to increase the caboose weight, like ballast on a ship. (I am not refering to the ponderous coal and iron-ore drags, which also had and still have caboose problems of their own.) It didn't take as many hand-brakes as you might think to control a fairly lightweight string of freight cars. The heavier a unit is, the more braking power it can apply and the greater the retardation and the less likelihood of sliding wheels. An iron or steel wheel sliding on steel rails travels farther than if it were revolving slowly.

Most waycars of yesteryear had three different brakes: one on each end and the third in the cupola. All were opposed. That is,

Two classic caboose scenes on the old New York, Ontario & Western line photographed around 1890. The little four-wheel crummy carried a small peek-a-boo cupola and flag holders on all four corners. What appears to be electric tail lights are kerosene operated marker lamps with a manually operated color disk system for signal and route identification. In the scene below, a caboose coach on the Northern District near the town of Norwich.—GERALD M. BEST COLLECTION

A caboose hop on the Bloomfield, Kentucky, branch of the Louisville & Nashville, circa 1902. The unusual caboose is obviously a converted boxcar. Note the bench mounted on top the hack.—L & N RAILWAY

any one of them, if tightened, would pull against the other two. Brakemen often used this principle to strengthen their caboose's braking power. When a car immediately ahead of them had a rear brake-staff, they would unbolt the chain from their own brake-staff and, with an additional length of chain fixed for that purpose, join the caboose brake-chain to the one on the car ahead.

Thus in applying their cupola brake they would also set the other car's brake at the same time. The brakes on these two cars, operated simultaneously and in conjunction with the engine's brakes, were enough to stop a train under ordinary circumstances. Many a time, as a young brakeman, I rode over an entire division without once getting out of the cupola.

During the long-gone era when engineers were regularly assigned steam locomotives, often with their names painted outside under the cab windows, and took pride in keeping them spic and span, numerous conductors with a lot of seniority likewise were assigned cabooses in which they felt a proprietary interest. Some conductors even had their names lettered on their waycars. A friend of mine recalls seeing in 1912 in the Southern Railway yards at Danville, Kentucky, a Southern caboose with a skipper's name painted boldly in white on a black background, glass-covered and surrounded by a frame about four feet long by eight inches deep, on both sides of the car. That name was really conspicuous. But the practice of painting names on cabooses was never widespread. It may have been started in the first place to emulate the engineers.

Years ago, numerous cabooses were assigned to me on a semipermanent basis but I never had my name painted on one. The few instances of this custom that I know of were probably due not to company policy but to the personal initiative of the men involved. Regardless of names, the assigned cars were usually kept freshly painted and scrubbed. A few were trimmed with curtains and other homelike accessories, a practice which most railroaders regard as "sissy." But even today many caboose walls, especially around the conductor's desk, are spotted with family photographs, newspaper or magazine clippings, and pin-up girls.

I recall having seen several waycars trimmed with evergreen for Yuletide, and even now trainmen occasionally cut down a Christmas tree in the big woods beyond the right-of-way fence and take it home in the caboose. It used to be fairly common many years ago for a crummy to sport flags and sometimes bunting on Memorial Day, Flag Day, or the 4th of July. This practice dated back to the more leisurely yesterdays when a caboose might be coupled behind old wooden coaches for a railroad employes' picnic. Now and then the engine also was decorated for a picnic run.

In the late 1800s', if a freight conductor "went to glory" in a train wreck his crummy might be solemnly draped with black crepe for 30 days. Casey Jones's widow once said that she remembered its being done on the Illinois Central in Tennessee and Mississippi, but that the practice was never widespread and didn't last long because of the depressing effect it had on other crews and because the brass collars regarded it as bad publicity for the company.

The "little red caboose" was not necessarily red. Not by a damsite! I have seen them just about every color of the rainbow except purple or gold. White wasn't so popular, though; it was too hard to keep clean. Today all Canadian National cabooses are painted bright orange—for greater visibility, which is important for long trains clearing a siding or rumbling over a grade crossing. With a glossy finish, these paint jobs wear well. However, the CNR underframes are still standard boxcar red. In the old days and on some roads, mostly shortlines, skippers to whom waycars were assigned could paint or decorate them any way they chose— within reason, of course.

I recall the case of John Johns, a husky, blue-eyed, and loud-voiced New York Central conductor who ran freight on the Hudson Division. Johnny had a creative mind. He wrote fiction stories for nationally-circulated magazines and aspired to become "the great American railroad novelist." For years his caboose carried a battered old Oliver typewriter and he worked on manuscripts at times when train operation did not require his full attention. Above all, he disliked conformity. Shortly before he died, in the late 1930's, he got in bad with his division superintendent by painting a pretty silver trim on "his" caboose. Johnny was proud of the job. But apparently the brass collar did not have an equally artistic eye. He ordered the frustrated conductor to restore the

Christmas Eve in a New Haven Railroad caboose.
All the comforts of home.—NEW HAVEN RAILROAD

Because of its unique status in the roster of railroad equipment, the narrow gauge caboose achieved an individuality unshared by the modern crummy with its automatic oil heaters, bay windows and electric lights. In this scene, a D&RGW caboose tags along behind an Alamosa bound freight east of Durango, Colorado.—JOHN KRAUSE

It's a warm day in the fall of 1952. The sound of mining fills the air at Monarch, Colorado, as the daily Denver & Rio Grande Western narrow gauge mine run starts the long haul down to Salida.—PHIL HASTINGS *(Below)* Colorado & Southern No. 68 and caboose No. 1003 in Clear Creek Canyon on the last narrow gauge run to Empire, Colorado, January 30, 1939.—RICHARD H. KINDIG

company property to its normal drab color on his own time and at his own expense.

"Luckily, they didn't lay me off without pay," Johnny said afterward. "The trouble with railroads today is that they don't encourage originality or initiative."

This may be true, but caboose designing long ago showed some variety. Bunks were built singly or two tiers high. Others, the swinging type, folded up against the ceiling like Pullman berths. In the densely populated East, with its access to hotels, boarding-houses, and YMCA's, less attention was paid to caboose bunks than in the prairie, desert, or mountain country. Down in the Southeast, where I spent many interesting years as a boomer trainman and later as a Southern Pacific "home guard," we had little facilities for eating and sleeping other than in the waycar. Its comforts looked solid enough then.

Generally speaking, the same situation applies to railroads all over the world where freight trains run long distances through sparsely-populated areas. Cabooses on the Trans-Siberian Rail-way, for example, provide eating and sleeping facilities comparable to those on the Santa Fe and Canadian Pacific, but are not used in mixed passenger and freight trains.

Western and southern Europe, however, have no "wide-open spaces" in the North American, Russian, or Australian sense. The countries are smaller, more compact, and more closely peopled. Even the long-distance freight runs tend to be shorter and there is little, if any, need for train crews to enjoy the comforts of home while trundling "goods," or merchandise, let's say from Liverpool to London. So the history and techniques of their cabooses for the most part are quite different from those I have known.

On British Railways the caboose is called a "goods brake-van" and the trainman in charge of it is a "guard." The guard is really a brakeman. He does not have the authority, prestige, or duties of a North American train conductor. When a British train is rolling over the road, its boss, if you must use the word, is the locomotive driver—subject, of course, to trackside signals and operating rules. The chief purpose of the brake-van is not to provide a home on the rails for trainmen nor a traveling office for the guard but to ensure that if a coupling should break in two or a drawbar be pulled out,

British version of the caboose—their standard brake-van. Note the small bay window, tail-lamp painted white and the two side lamps which permit the engine crew to see if their train is still following at night. *(Below)* Another brake-van with shock-absorbing space in front and back of the car body.—BRITISH RAILWAYS

Great Western Railway brake-van on a local shunt.—F. W. TRITTENBACH

the guard will take care of the trailing portion and apply a hand brake. Also, when the train is running normally through up and down grades the guard on the brake-van applies hand-braking on the down grade to present undue drawbar strain—in other words, to avoid what the British term "drawbar snatching." But the drivers, as a rule, try to run their trains without the aid of rear-end braking, just in case a guard should be negligent on the down grade.

The trend on British Railways is to get rid of brake-vans. If they should do so, it is likely that the guards on freight trains would ride in the rear cars of diesel-electric locomotives and be relieved of such caboose-like jobs as lighting coal stoves and trimming side and tail lamps (marker lights). Nearly all British brake-vans are four-wheelers, although the former Great Western Railway used six-wheelers, which are now extinct. At one time, until about 1954, some British brake-vans were equipped with sandboxes and associated levers so that, should the wheels skid, a trainman could spread a carpet of sand beneath them. On the

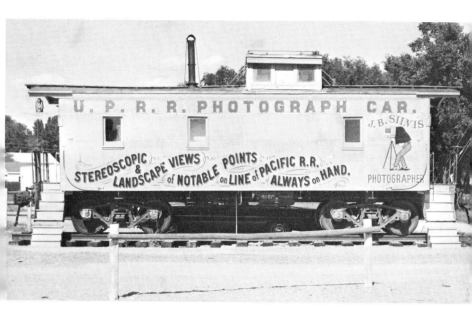

Replica of the original Union Pacific photographic car now stands in a parking lot on Front St., Ogallala, Nebraska.—JIM SEACREST

Southern Region, a number of electric locomotives have been converted for use as brake-vans.

Most European countries no longer use the caboose or brake-van. Instead, their freight cars have a rear ladder which a trainman mounts to apply a hand-brake when the need arises. In Germany the caboose, or *Gueterzugpackwagen* (literally translated "freight-train baggage car"), was introduced in the 1840's when the first non-mixed freight trains went into service. As in Britain and elsewhere in western and southern Europe, where distances are short, the German caboose has never been the freight crew's home for long stretches of time but only for hours. Therefore, its interior is much simpler than those of North American waycars.

Its main feature is a room for the conductor, with an elevated seat to permit him to look over the car tops, and seating space (not bunks) for the switching crews. The rest of the caboose is just like a baggage room with sliding doors. In fact, long ago, it actually carried baggage. Before the air-brake was installed it also

45

A Boston & Maine crossing tender gives the train crew a friendly highball as a fast freight rushes along Railroad Avenue at Greenwood, Mass.—BOSTON & MAINE

served as a warming place for brakemen in winter time.

Unlike North American practice, the *Gueterzugpackwagen* has always been coupled directly behind the engine. Today's long-distance freight trains on the German Federal Railroad do not carry switching crews, because they run from one yard to another, in each of which personnel are available to handle all movements. Only the conductor, with his freight papers, rides the long-distance caboose. Local freights have two or three men aboard, but little provision is made for their comfort, as the run lasts only two or three hours.

Today, the caboose is almost obsolete in Europe. None have been built in West Germany since World War II. Old two-axle passenger coaches are replacing them. West Germany's diesel- and electric-powered freights no longer have cabooses. The train conductor rides the locomotive, along with the engineer (there is no fireman). Many German steam locomotives have a little cabin built near the middle of the coal tender. It has big windows and is heated in cold weather. This is the conductor's office.

On the old Bavarian State Railways each caboose was equipped with huge ornate beer steins for the crew, Bavaria being noted for its beer. One of the duties of the youngest switchman riding the caboose was to refill those steins often at station stops. Although Rule G of American railroads forbids the drinking of alcoholic beverages by employees on duty, trainmen in the United States enjoyed many other comforts over the years and their cabooses had much more variety than those in Europe.

To the lay observer, all oldtime cabooses in North America may have seemed pretty much alike; but there was a wide diversity in types, especially on shortlines and logging roads. The trucks varied from close together to far apart; some had front and rear platforms without overhang while others had overhang without platforms. I remember one caboose that shot up from the platform to the cupola like a miniature skyscraper. And not long ago the Bangor & Aroostook boasted a type of waycar with an airhorn on top that was used to signal the head end.

The main difference between North American cabooses and most of those in other parts of the globe was, I think, caboose cookery. That subject is taken up in my next chapter.

A few miles east of Burlington, Quebec, Canada, a local passenger train passes a drag freight steaming along on a parallel track.—JOHN KRAUSE

In bygone days caboose cookery was both a necessity and a choice. Here a Santa Fe Railway brakeman cuts up and cooks a batch of spuds on a small caboose stove.—DONALD DUKE

THREE

Caboose Cookery

GONE are the days when a conductor wired his trainmaster: "Brakeman Horton ill. Send man to relieve him. Must be good cook." The necessity for preparing and eating meals in cabooses has been cut to a minimum by the rapid growth in population, with a constantly increasing number of restaurants and lunch counters, in addition to faster freight schedules and fewer hours on duty.

Things were different in the "Golden Age of Railroading," as it is fondly called. I can still smell and taste, in my mind, the bacon and eggs and potatoes I fried and ate in cabooses, the Mulligan stew, the turtle chowder—in fact, the thousands of satisfying breakfasts, dinners, and suppers prepared by or for me and shared by other crew members on waycars throughout the West, the Midwest, and Southwest. I once spent more than a year in work trains on the desert. During that time the entire crew ate every meal, except on Sundays, in the caboose. We had pretty fair eats, too. But no fresh meat; there was no facility for keeping it. The canned meat we had went mighty well mixed with vegetables in the form of baked hash.

One dish we often enjoyed was baked beans. For this we worked out a cooking scheme I've never seen elsewhere. We cleaned a five-gallon oil can, cut it in two, and trimmed the top half just enough to fit into the lower part. Thus we created a false bottom which we punched full of holes. A handful of iron nuts kept it from contact with the boiler's bottom, making in effect a double-boiler of the whole affair. So if we had to leave the crummy for a while, with the beans on the stove, we didn't worry about their sticking to the bottom and scorching. We'd turn them, when fully cooked, into a shallow baking-pan, cover the top with sliced bacon, and set that pan in the oven to crisp the bacon. Those beans were fit for anybody's palate.

A typical caboose would carry one or more hams, a huge side of bacon, sacks of flour and sugar, a bushel of potatoes, some onions, ample coffee, and canned goods. Four or five large wheat sacks filled with coal would be lashed to the running board and there would be a triple supply of kerosene. It took a heap of groceries to feed five or six hungry men three meals a day for perhaps four or five days, and a lot of fuel to keep that crummy heated and lighted, especially in winter time. If you were caught short of supplies just once, you could bet it would never happen again.

Bill Moore, as parlor brakeman, did the cooking for a Great Northern crew that worked over the Cascade Mountains and through the old Cascade Tunnel at Wellington, Washington, in the winter of 1908 when the snow often piled up 10 or 15 feet. "We lived on the caboose," he recalls, "and bought all our groceries at Maloney's store in Skykomish, splitting the bill three ways each pay day, and we stocked up a-plenty because we never knew when we'd get stuck behind a slide. I'd never start on a trip without three dozen eggs, a big slab of bacon or a ham, a sack of spuds, lots of beans and coffee, canned milk, a roast, beef for stew, onions, and flour for biscuits and hotcakes.

"Sometimes we'd be snowed in for three days straight, in which case the grub also fed two engineers and a fireman. They each gave me 30 cents a meal, which I put in a can to buy more groceries. We also kept a gallon of good whiskey on the caboose. This was a violation of rules, but the trainmaster would look at the moon when we had a shot, and we did the same for him."

In bygone days caboose cookery was both a necessity and a choice. It permitted you to eat when you were hungry and not have to wait, often many long and weary hours, until you arrived at the terminal. Back in the dangerous years before Congress enacted the 16-hour law, the "hog law," which limited the number of hours that train and engine crews could be on duty continuously, it was common practice for a freight to be tied up on the road waiting what seemed like endless hours for a relief crew to show up. At such times caboose cookery was real nice.

Even today and even in the East, there are places where winter weather, isolation, or other rugged conditions makes it necessary for crews to eat their meals in the waycar. Such an area is the Adirondack Mountains, which in winter is called the icebox of New York State. There snowdrifts can be 15 feet deep, with the mercury at 20 below. The members of one New York Central crew regarded chocolate pudding as the ideal dessert and dubbed their rear brakeman, Martin Fraser, "the chocolate pudding king" because of his skill in preparing that dish. He had a way with Java, too. First he'd throw a half-dozen handfuls of coffee into the pot and add water. Then the concoction would stand overnight and he'd boil it in the morning, and when you drank it—*Wow!* The caboose breakfasts on that run seldom varied. It was a standing joke to ask Fraser, "What are we having for breakfast?" His answer was generally the same: "Coffee, bacon and eggs, toast, and jam." That stuff must have tasted good on mornings when the caboose windows were frosted over.

My friend G. H. Harris, past president of the Order of Railway Conductors and Brakemen, recalls the days when he was a conductor. "My regular assigned flagman was of Italian descent and an excellent cook," he told me. "There was a tacit understanding on the division that no other brakeman, even one with more seniority, would be especially welcome on my caboose if he got there by bumping my good cook. I often ate better in the caboose than I did in my own home.

"During the years of World War II, when some food items normally could be gotten only through ration stamps, my flagman negotiated and obtained them by his cooking and bargaining ability. We often had military equipment in our train that required a troop escort, usually an officer and a few enlisted men riding in a caboose placed ahead of our regular waycar. By the very nature of our assignment, the military personnel often had to go many hours and even days while in transit without getting good meals or even hot coffee. We'd supply them with a huge kettle of stew, Italian spaghetti, or some other 'home-cooked' delicacy. It was a rare treat for them to break their usual dreary 'tin-can meals' as they traveled across the country. Our goodwill efforts frequently led to the stocking of our caboose with certain foods that were hard to get on the civilian market."

Many years ago, when bush camps were set up along every few miles of the Canadian Pacific right-of-way and their cooks were lonely, it was common practice for a passing freight to give them current mail-order catalogs. These, in turn, resulted in orders from the catalogs, which a trainman would mail at the nearest post office. The trackside "chefs" showed their appreciation by giving the railroaders occasional slabs of bacon, big fragrant loaves of camp bread, pies, and man-sized cookies. Other contributors to the CPR caboose meals included commercial travelers, or "drummers" who often rode freight trains before the highways were opened.

Some crew men stocked their caboose cupboards with food brought from home on a *pro rata* basis: home-canned fruits and vegetables, dried lima beans, hominy, and so on. A big, zinc-lined, sawdust-insulated box often took the place of a refrigerator. Trackside farms were regarded as legitimate foraging grounds for fresh produce. An unwritten law placed the first four or five rows of fruits and vegetables nearest the track at the disposal of freight crews. When corn was ripe, for example, the train would stop long enough for the caboose riders to grab a couple of armfuls. Sometimes, but not very often, you paid for the green groceries with a fair sum of money laid on a corner fence post where the farmer could easily find it. One oldtimer recalls the custom of buying freshly-killed chickens from a farmer. Today the crews on that same run sometimes buy fresh eggs from local farmers, but the only chicken they eat in the caboose comes out of a can or is pre-cooked at home by a brakeman's wife, to save time.

Few boomers were inclined to pay for edibles they could get free. My friend the late "Haywire Mac" (Harry K. McClintock), brakeman, switchman, and minstrel, occasionally related his experiences in magazine articles, and this is what he wrote about foraging for caboose menus:

"Memory harks back to my youth as a boomer, when a whole year of railroading had only 12 pay days, when 50 or 60 bucks collected in the pay-car was a pretty fair month's wages, when you could buy fresh eggs for as little as 12 Indian pennies a dozen, and when a good glass of lager beer set you back a Liberty nickel. For about 48 hours after pay day, rarely longer, we boomers were plutocrats, but we were always broke before the money-wagon came around again. Some guys were content to get along on what could be procured in grocery stores for cash or credit while others of us remembered that Providence was inclined to smile on a hustler.

"In those days you could pick up quite a few delicacies free of charge; and probably even now, by giving thought to the problem, you can find ways of replenishing your larder on the non-payment basis. This applies only to those who cook caboose meals. I admit that the desert divisions of the Southwest offer scant reward for an industrious forager, but the territory east of the Mississippi should be almost as good as it ever was.

"On the old Pittsburgh, Fort Wayne & Chicago (now part of the Pennsy system) I 'broke' partners with Artie Fletcher, a tall rangy lad. At all times a search of our crummy would have revealed a .22 rifle, a shotgun, fishing-rods, tackle, and occasionally a large minnow skein which, after dark, often landed fish bigger than minnows. As we headed into a siding in the brush and bramble country we first looked over our train as a matter of course. Then, instead of taking to the cushions for a snooze or a gabfest, we'd drop a line or two into the nearest creek in the hope of picking up an unwary bass. Or if it was fall or winter we'd be out in the stubble fields along the track in search of rabbits or quail.

"In spring, when the white suckers were running, Artie would get down into the creek, drive the fish into the tangled grass roots under an overhanging bank, and grab them with his hands. In midsummer I have seen him use the same method to capture snapping turtles, and as a result of wayside foraging we cooked many a mess of delicious fried turtle or turtle soup.

"Almost any pasture was good for mushrooms. There are supposed to be 30 or more species of edible fungi, but I can't distinguish more than four of them. Three of this number—the spongy mushrooms, the 'shaggy mane,' and the type with a pink underside—grow in the spring. The fourth one, the puffball, come along about summertime, but comparatively few people are aware it is edible. This kind, when dry, is known as 'the devil's snuffbox,' but if you are lucky enough to stumble across them when they are fresh you'll find them good eating. To cook, peel off the outer layer, cut the rest into slices like eggplant, dip into egg batter, and fry until golden brown. But don't go gathering fungi until you've had a few instructions from someone who knows the difference between mushrooms and toadstools. The latter are plenty lethal.

"There is still an abundance of cornfields, and to my way of thinking the old field corn is just as tasty as any fancy sweet corn. No caboose in which meals are cooked need be without a supply of fruit from the time that early-harvest apples start to ripen; and when the farmers are loading potatoes it should be a cinch for a fast talker to 'promote' a bushel or so along any country-town team track.

"Farmers used to plant the watermelon patch a considerable distance from the house so that the pollen from cucumbers and squash vines would not get mixed in with the big green-stripers. Furthermore, you can pick blackberries and raspberries along the fence rows and clumps of elderberry bushes in almost every pasture. At least you *could*—in the days before superhighways.

"Take along a .22 when you go berrying and perhaps you can knock over a groundhog. The young ones make a delicious pot-roast. If you are braking on through freight on runs where you handle an occasional carload of poultry, carry a few packages of egg noodles in the caboose cupboard at all times. Usually the guy in charge of the chicken car (if there is one in your consist) will surreptitiously donate a fat fowl or two, provided you guarantee to invite him to the feast.

56

"So far, this little essay has dealt with foraging methods that are more or less ethical. It is probably best to stay on the safe side; so we will not mention the quaint old boomer custom of knocking a hoop up on a whiskey barrel and driving a soapy nail through a stave. The soap made the nail easy to withdraw and, if you happened to have provided a bucket, you could catch the resultant amber stream to be bottled for future reference.

"After that, a match plugged the hole, and the hoop covered all signs of tampering when you drove it back into place again. (However, in these decadent days they almost never ship barreled whiskey in less than carload lots, and present-day railroaders don't drink—much.) And we will say nothing of the savage nature of oldtime farmyard fowls when they got near a railroad right-of-way. Such birds have been known to attack unarmed brakemen rather viciously. Naturally, the poor shack had no recourse but to kill the pugnacious Plymouth Rock in self-defense.

"The old Fort Wayne road ran through the village of Lakeville, Ohio, where the Pennsy put up thousands of tons of ice every winter for the re-icing of refrigerator cars. Lakeville had a telegraph office and sidings, but the sidings were seldom used, as the switches were not controlled by interlocking. One of my braking partners on this road, a lad named Kehoe, was a pretty good 'promoter.' We had long harbored nefarious designs against a certain barnyard full of fat poultry. Much time passed before we got a chance at them, but finally our luck seemed to be good. We picked up an order to pull in at Lakeside for a couple of manifest freights that were running on short time.

"By pre-arrangement, we met that night at about the middle of the train, jerked our lanterns out, and headed for the chicken house. The night was just about perfect: no moon, a cloudy sky, and darker than the inside of a tunnel. Easing through the barbed-wire right-of-way fence, we crossed a pasture field and crawled up to that chicken house with the caution of an Apache Indian. Reaching the door, we gingerly pulled it open—and then suddenly all bedlam broke loose! Besides the chickens, that coop sheltered about a dozen big gray geese and they cut out with more din than a boiler factory.

"As we scudded across the pasture we heard a noise from the house like someone stumbling downstairs. A voice shouted some unkind words, a screen door slammed, and then we hit that barbed-wire fence. We got through it by leaving part of our clothing on the barbs, and tumbled down over the bank just as the unreasonable farmer cut loose at us from the front porch with both barrels of his shotgun. The old boy couldn't see us in the darkness. He was only shooting at the noise we made, but he wasn't doing badly at that, for the charge whistled uncomfortably close to our heads and a shower of buckshot hit the boxcar like a shovelful of gravel.

"We barely had time to find and light our lanterns on the opposite side of the train when the irate chicken-owner came up and found us doctoring a phony hotbox. Of course, we were innocent of any evil intention. The attempted raid on his poultry yard must have been the work of unscrupulous hoboes. We even helped him to frisk the train in a vain effort to find them. But even to this day I'm not certain he swallowed our alibi. That wise old agriculturist had a baleful look in his eye and he stayed with us until we pulled out. When I finally closed the switch and caught the caboose, he was stationed right at the switch-stand, still nursing his shotgun."

Not all poultry raiders got off so easily. One cold November night many years ago, in a drizzling rain, Union Pacific extra No. 2498 arrived at LaSalle, Colorado, and left shortly afterward with a string of empties. The conductor, whom I will call Goog, was walking alongside the drag checking car numbers when he spied a turkey hiding quietly in the weeds out of the rain. After glancing around and seeing nobody, he lifted his lantern in a quick highball. As the train began to pull out, Goog grabbed the turkey and carried it triumphantly into the caboose.

"How's this for a Thanksgiving feast?" he asked the rear brakeman. "Get me a piece of cord and we'll tie him up."

When the slow train reached Dent, a red board stopped it. Before the flagman could get off to pick up orders, a man wearing a tin badge climbed into the caboose and introduced himself as a deputy sheriff. The turkey was squawking at the end of a tether. Its owner had witnessed the theft and phoned the sheriff's office. The deputy drove over from LaSalle, seized the indignant bird, and collected $7.50 from the crestfallen conductor.

"Five dollars fine," he said, "and two-fifty for expenses."

But that wasn't all. Upon arriving at Denver, Goog was called into the trainmaster's office and pulled out of service for 30 days. His loss of pay plus the $7.50 raised the price of that untasted turkey to $199. Which reminds me of another Haywire Mac story:

"I was braking on local Pennsy freight between Alliance and Mansfield, Ohio, when Yuletide rolled around. Business was so good that we were told to work on Christmas day, so we planned a spread in the crummy. One of our gang had won a turkey in a raffle and we paid a town cook to roast it for us the day before, with oyster dressing and other trimmings. All we had to do was warm up the meal and serve.

"We decided to tie up at Millbrook, which had a water plug and coal chute, long enough to do justice to the feast. Just before reaching that town we coupled into a bunch of chain-ups at Wooster—five cars, chained together—and there must have been 30 feet of slack in the rear. As we pulled up to the coal chute, the turkey was on the stove in a giant roasting pan, steaming hot and filling the air with its fragrance. Our potatoes had been mashed, the coffee made, and the gravy was ready. The hind shack set the table.

"But the idiotic hogger must have forgotten those chain-ups. He spotted his ten-wheeler while the crummy was still making about ten miles an hour and the slack ran out with a *wham* you could have heard for a mile. Our flagman landed on the seat of his britches against the front door. The coalbox caught some of the banquet while the rest was distributed between the rear brakeman and the floor. Grease, turkey, cranberry sauce, and broken dishes were strewn about.

"The parlor brakeman arose, dripping with gravy and standing in a pool of Java, to deliver an oration on the subject of hogheads in general and ours in particular. He spoke at length on their maternal ancestry, their present conduct, and their probable fate at the hands of an outraged universe. The con and I stood at attention with our hats off. It was that good. After a while, we ate ham and eggs at the local beanery—all except the craven hogger. He had the fireman take him a ham sandwich and coffee over to the engine."

Incidentally, engine crews rarely got in on caboose meals, since it would have involved a major disruption of the schedule to stop the train long enough for them to go back to the waycar and eat. Besides, hostility between the engineer and train crew was not uncommon, as you might gather from Haywire Mac's story. This feeling is exemplified by a bit of doggerel entitled *Put the Hogger in the Crummy*, written by B. H. Terry, an old freight conductor:

> Let me sit on the right-hand side,
>   A-hold of the throttle and Johnson bar,
> And make our rough old hogger ride
>   At the other end in the old waycar,
> Just watch him try to stay in the hack
>   When I start the train with the air and slack
> And hear him holler when his head I drove
>   Right in behind the crummy stove.
>
> As the train goes into the sag,
>   Knock him out with the slack in that drag
> And let him lay there on the floor,
>   Afraid to stand for fear he'd get more.
> I'd head right in on the longest track
>   And cut her off a long way back.
> When the hogger walks in, to him I'd say:
>   "Well, how was the ride you got today?"

The engineer's rough handling of trains, especially at meal time in the caboose, was one of the reasons why they usually had to bring lunch from home, in the old days, rather than share in the trainmen's freshly cooked food. Haywire Mac's experience at Millbrook that Christmas day reminds me of the time I was braking for conductor Ed Suell on the Southern Pacific. Ed invariably wore a stiff-bosomed shirt, which was not uncommon around the turn of

The conductor had a way with making Java. First he'd throw a half-dozen handfuls of coffee into the pot and add water. The concoction would then stand overnight and he'd boil it in the morning, and when you drank it . . . wow!—NEW YORK CENTRAL

the century, and a turn-down celluloid collar but no necktie, and seldom buttoned his vest. Our eastward extra had just headed in at Mammoth, California. It was early evening and Ed was making supper.

I closed the switch, caught the crummy, and signaled the head end. Then I went inside and told Ed, "The order board is red," meaning that the operator had a flimsy for us. In those days nearly all train orders were "31" forms, the kind that the skipper had to sign for. Ed had set a pan of fried spuds on the cupola floor and his hands were full of dough, for he was making biscuits. So he said: "Go to the telegraph office, Bill, and sign for whatever he's got."

Our train, by the way, was pulled by one of the huge steam locomotives, equipped with independent, or "straight air," brakes, that the SP had bought a short time before. Most of the engineers were still unfamiliar with those brakes and had no conception of what effect their full application would have on the rest of the train; but it didn't take them long to be informed, in lurid and profane language, by irate skippers.

Our engineer, Davis, hadn't learned—yet. Just as I opened the caboose door he moved the train forward a little. The jerk rammed my head and shoulders through the glass door. It tumbled Ed backward in such a way that his shoulders struck my knee and his head was thrust between my legs, later hitting the floor with a solid thump. The pan of hot murphies sailed through the air. It turned upside down, lit on Ed's belt buckle, slid up his white stiff bosom, and veered off to one side, leaving a trail of grease en route. The pain of his bump made Ed forget the biscuit dough. He grabbed his sparse hair with both hands. At that instant the hot grease from the spuds soaked through his shirt and Ed came to his feet with a yell like a Comanche Indian.

If I live to be a hundred—which seems likely at my present age —I'll never forget that sight: Ed's hair decorated with dough, his shirt bosom bedaubed with greasy hieroglyphics, and his eyes glinting like fire. The language he used on that occasion must have been pretty close to the oratory Mac heard at Millbrook. And while I am thinking of Mac again, here is a piece he wrote about caboose cookery:

"It must all be done on top of the stove, although some roads in the South equip their cabooses with a regular ship's range, oven and all. This may be because Southerners go for cornbread and biscuits in a big way. I have seen such ranges also in Western Pacific crummies and oil stoves on the Espee, but in each case the crew had installed them at their own expense. So we'll assume that practically all caboose cookery is done on top of the stove.

"The first requirement is a kettle—not a tall narrow pot but a low squatty one that won't upset easily when the hogger makes a rough stop. A tight flanged lid will keep it from falling off. I used to pick up a light piece of chain and fasten it to the roof directly above the stove. You can then suspend your kettle so that it rests lightly on the stove. If the yard crew should take a notion to switch your caboose track while dinner is cooking, your Mulligan will remain right side up. When buying a skillet for the caboose, get a cast-iron or heavy steel kind. The lightweight variety will scorch your chow before it is heated through.

"An old-fashioned Dutch oven lets you turn out pot-roasts fit for a king. Just get it hot, use plenty of grease, and sear your meat well, turning it often. After that add a couple quarts of water, two or three onions, a carrot and, if you like, a bit of garlic. Then clap the lid on and let 'er simmer slowly for about two hours. Put more water in from time to time if needed. About 20 minutes before meal time add your peeled spuds—and before sitting down to eat be sure to invite the worthy brother who is riding with you.

"Round steak should be fried; but pan-broil a good sirloin or a porterhouse. Use no grease. Just dust the pan with salt, slap in your sirloin or porterhouse, and turn it when the under side is done. Better cook your potatoes first and have them ready. If there is a lot of ashes under the grates, bury your spuds down deep and bake them.

"Among my favorite ways of cooking spuds is the 'caboose-track fry.' Slice your potatoes and onions, put them into a skillet with plenty of grease, and fry until half done, covering with a tight lid. This recipe beats the spuds served in a beanery. Of course, if you don't aim to stay on the job much longer than next pay day you won't want to fix up the crummy with an elaborate outfit of

Eating in the caboose ain't fancy, but who cares?
It's the food that really counts.—NEW HAVEN RR

On many cabooses, newspapers serve as convenient and disposable tablecloths. With a steaming plate of food, a piece of fresh-baked pie, and a hot cup of coffee, who cares about luxury? Trouble is, the railroad forgot to install an automatic dishwasher.—NEW YORK CENTRAL

culinary utensils. In that case you could always make a Mulligan in a five-gallon oil can. I have even cooked stew in a new 'dope' bucket before it is used to hold material for treating hotboxes.

"To make a frying-pan, cut the ends out of a five-gallon oil can and split it down one corner. Now you have a nice piece of tin. Flatten it on the floor, double it, and flatten it again. Then turn the edges up about an inch all around and you will have a fair-sized skillet with a double bottom that will not scorch your grub easily.

"You can broil a steak right on top of the stove. Just wash the top off good with a hunk of waste. Then get her hot, but not too hot; sprinkle your stove lid with salt, and slap on your steak. I learned that one from an old Chinese cook who had a 'pie-card' sign up at Gerlach, Nevada. His joint was noted for fine juicy steaks and that's the way he cooked 'em. If the steak was cut a little thin he'd set a flat-iron on top to keep the edges from curling up."

When the aroma of a simmering dinner fills the car, the railroaders waste no time digging in. With a steaming plate of food, a piece of home-baked pie, and a hot beverage under their belts, they're filled with new vigor—that is, until someone eyes the stack of dishes that need attention. Then there's a slight hesitation. At length one of the brakemen drags out the dishpan and tackles the job. The other grabs a towel and dries. Sometimes the conductor helps to the extent of passing out the dish towel.

On many cabooses, newspapers serve as convenient and disposable tablecloths. The story is told of a Canadian Pacific trainman who was assigned to setting the table as his K.P. duty but was not informed that 30 issues of the same newspaper had been left behind by an indifferent distributor. At the first meal the trainman spread the paper "tablecloth" and, according to the custom, read aloud the headlines and other choice items for discussion. At the second meal he remarked that he could have sworn he'd read this same paper before. When he learned the truth he groaned at the prospect of setting table for the next month with copies of the same newspaper.

Housewives who watch the competitive TV commercials today

for detergents and scouring powders are not likely to think of dishwashing in oldtime cabooses. But if they should, they'd probably visualize our pots and pans as far from spotless. In this connection, F. E. Brown was braking for the Santa Fe out of Slaton, Texas, one morning when he got a message to pick up some outfit cars at Snyder. At that time railroad laborers with their families used such cars as living quarters, but the women were not allowed to ride in them while the cars were being transferred from one location to another. Instead, they rode in cabooses. One of them, dressed in a pretty white linen suit, went into Brown's waycar. Brown got down from the cupola and began fixing something to eat.

The lady remarked, "I'll bet you make a mess while you are cooking."

In reply Brown picked up his skillet, casually wiped off any dust that may have accumulated on it, and set it on her lap.

"My God," she yelped, "you have ruined my dress!"

"Madame," he said, "if it is spoiled I'll buy you a new one."

She seemed afraid to touch the skillet, so the brakeman took it off her lap, and she looked for stains on her white garment but there were none.

"Mr. Brown," she said, "I'll have to admit my own skillet isn't *that* clean."

After they had finished eating, the lady conceded that his cooking was a lot better than she had expected. Another thing that interested her was: how do train crews prepare meals on a caboose while the train is running around curves or over uneven track? How do they keep their cooking utensils from being jolted off the stove?

Haywire Mac has told us how he solved that problem by using a chain attached to the saucepan. One caboose stove I had on the Southern Pacific was equipped with a railing or fence around the edge to keep low vessels like skillets from sliding off. Larger pots were protected by a chain or two, or maybe wires, each with a hook on the lower end, fastened to the wooden ceiling. You improvise such precautions after you have had a Mulligan or a hot custard deposited on the floor.

A popular dish in caboose meals was an occasional fish of

impressive size. It was oven-baked, well salted, and basted now and then with drippings. One conductor on a Great Northern work train kept a stew boiling steadily in a five-gallon pan. After going home he'd return with a hunk of elk or venison which was getting a bit fragrant and toss it into the stew. This potent mess is said to have contained all the known vitamins plus a few others. The skipper also carried a shotgun, with which he added a few ducks and pheasants to the bill-of-fare. One day he lost a suit of underwear. The crew members wondered whether or not it had got into the stew. A variation on this was hamburger (re-named Salisbury steak, for patriotic reasons, during World War II). An old boomer trainman and engineer, "Windy" Werner Derden, gave me this recipe for it:

> To make a dozen large bun-sized patties, take 2 pounds of ground lean beef, 10 slices of rye or whole wheat bread, and garlic, salt, and pepper to suit the taste. Wet the bread; squeeze out most of the water. Break an egg into it so it will brown nicely. Mix well. Brown in butter. Then add water, cover with a lid, and let it steam. Remove the patties and, if desired, make cream gravy in the butter.

Windy also supplied the following tasty recipe for caboose turtle chowder, enough to make two meals for a crew of five:

> Boil and take the bones out of 5 or 6 pounds of turtle or cat-fishmeat. Save the stock or broth. Dice and brown one pound of salt pork in the pit where the charcoal is to be cooked. Dice 2 pounds of Irish potatoes, 2 pounds of carrots, one pound of onions, and one bell-shaped green pepper or pimiento, and boil until tender. Then add a small can of tomato paste and stir while bringing to a boil. Add salt and pepper to suit your taste.

Pie is a favorite dessert on the road, as it is elsewhere, especially apple pie; but in most of the cabooses I knew rice custard was liked best and served most frequently. Here is our recipe:

> When the rice is about half cooked, dump in a half-pound of seedless raisins and enough sugar to please your palate. After it is well done, place the concoction in a baking-pan. Then

68

Long ago, most cabooses were heated by coal or oil stoves; this one on the Norfolk Southern burns wood. Note the pile of fresh-cut wood on the platform.—H. REID *(Below)* The conductor hands grub aboard the caboose prior to a run on New York Central's Ottawa Division.— NEW YORK CENTRAL

add a custard made of eggs, butter, and canned milk, flavored with vanilla extract. Put the whole mess into the oven and bake until it is brown on top.

This, my friends, makes a dessert you will relish, if you aren't stingy with the butter and eggs. But hot dishes evoked the best talent in caboose cookery. Tom Reese, a Seaboard Air Line conductor with a ruddy face and blue eyes, was one of those with a high regard for hot meals. Tom, in fact, had a positive aversion to sandwiches.

"A doctor in Columbia, South Carolina, told me about 20 years ago that enough sandwiches would kill a man," he said. "Since that time I've eaten only three and I am trying to forget them. Now, you take the way we run, when we pull out of Hamlet for Andrews I chuck a little meat into the pot and some onions, small potatoes, and a couple of bunches of carrots. I season to taste with whatever is handy, put in enough water to float the vegetables, and bank the stove up to what would be a medium head of steam.

"Then I wire the top of the pot on tight with a coat-hanger and I slide it under my home-made railing over the stove so it won't upset. After that I won't look at it again till we go to eat. A Mulligan stew like that is pretty good. It sure makes the hogger thoughtful and kind. He won't go bumping a string of cars up against the crummy, 'cause I am the man who says what the seating arrangement will be at this table when the dinner bell rings."

Caboose tableware contrasted sharply with the kind used in dining cars. Many years ago, one night I was running the Southern Pacific's mountain local between Colton and Indio, California. My train headed into a siding at White Water (now Palm Springs) to wait for a meet with a "string of varnish," Number 9. Pretty soon the passenger train appeared, displaying signals for another section, and stopped on the main line beside the freight. Its brightly lighted windows made a pattern of golden oblongs on our boxcars. Passengers were reading on the other side of those windows, dozing, engaged in desultory conversation, or lingering over a late meal in the diner.

Aboard a Canadian Pacific Railway caboose rolling along at 50 m.p.h., conductor D. Washburn pours himself a cup of coffee during his lunch break. Note the caboose cast in the stove door.—PHIL HASTINGS

For a moment I watched them from the rear platform of my waycar. Then I stepped inside, filled a tin cup from the ever-present coffee pot that simmered aromatically on the stove, and turned to my desk to make an entry on my delay report. As I raised my eyes, I found myself looking directly into a dining-car window a little more than an arm's length away.

At the table sat a nice-looking young couple, apparently dawdling over their coffee, gazing back at me. The man said something to the girl. She smiled. They both raised their gleaming white cups and held them toward me as if in a toast. Not to be outdone, I grinned and lifted my tin cup to them. All three of us drank. Never before had Java tasted so good to me. The passenger train started to move and their window slid away. "Drinkers that pass in the night."

It was around that time, about 1915, that a westbound freight on the Espee's Los Angeles Division ran into a cloudburst. The track being washed out ahead, the skipper backed his freight into a siding at his rear. The same thing happened with a following passenger train. Thus the two trains stood on separate sidings, with the tracks washed out ahead, behind, and between them. The miles of track missing in that immediate area added up to about 13. This was in the desert—the sand, cactus, and rattlesnake country—many miles from the nearest town, and no help could be expected until the tracks were repaired.

On the third day the passenger train's diner ran out of food. A blue-uniformed brakeman walked up ahead through the glistening pools to the freight train to ascertain what provisions, if any, were available there. The freight consist included a carload of mixed groceries, but a side-wash had eddied under that car and the skipper feared that if it were moved it would turn over on one side. So he had his engine brought down the main line and she pushed the caboose onto the main with the aid of a stout pole that had been carried in the possum belly for such purposes. This operation is known as "poling."

Then, as the waycar stood opposite the load of edibles, his crew transferred some of the stuff into the crummy. After that it was backed as close to the passenger train as the washout permitted, while the dining car was moved as far up as possible, thus narrowing the gap between the two trains. Thereupon both train crews, assisted by the postal clerks and some of the male passengers, toted boxes, baskets, and cartons of groceries across "no-man's land" and into the diner, and nobody had to go hungry. Just another case of a caboose going to the rescue of stranded passengers!

On many runs a flood, landslide, or blizzard blocked the progress of a freight train I was riding. Nowadays the railroad companies use giant rotary plows to open a stretch of track piled high with snow, fast and efficiently, but I can recall the smaller, slower, and less efficient wedge plows that were operated for the same purpose long, long ago. Because of the possibility of such emergencies the freight crews, especially on Western roads, usually left their home terminal with a plentiful supply of "eatables" in the waycar.

For shorter runs we didn't carry so much food. Additions to the menu from unexpected sources—like Mrs. Gilbert Sproule, for example—were "pennies from heaven." Mrs. Sproule was the SP agent at West Orange, Calif., when I was braking on the Santa Ana night local. Because of her friendly disposition, we fellows on the crew often helped her with depot chores. Being an expert cook, she'd reciprocate our favors by giving us generous slices of the pies or cakes she baked. One evening when we pulled into West Orange we found two plump white ducks in a coop setting on a baggage truck on the station platform.

Said Mrs. Sproule: "If you boys will kill and pluck these ducks and leave them here on your return I'll cook them and you all can have a duck dinner with me."

That idea made our mouths water. The head brakeman volunteered to kill the web-footed birds and leave them in the caboose to be de-feathered by conductor "Slim" Harlin and me. Never having plucked a duck before, I knew nothing of the down that lays under its outer feathers, but I soon learned. We rolled out of West Orange with Slim and me on the rear platform scattering a snowstorm of white feathers behind us.

Well, I picked and picked until all the large feathers were off and then I came to the down, or pin feathers. Did you ever try to get the down off a duck? It's almost like pulling out one hair at a time. I worked at it every chance I got all the way to Los Angeles and most of the way back. Slim made a pretty fair job of his duck but we were fast approaching West Orange and mine was nowhere completed. In desperation I hung that blooming fowl by the neck to the safety rod in the cupola, lathered the carcass, and shaved it with my straight-edge razor. When I got through, it was as clean as a new china plate. Mrs. Sproule greeted us happily and complimented me on a fine job of picking. We enjoyed her roast dinner with all the trimmings that night, but a long time passed before I confessed how I had "picked" my duck.

Many years ago the caboose on all through freight trains of the Nashville, Chattanooga & St. Louis was equipped with a coop, built underneath the car and opposite the possum belly. That coop usually had a few live chickens in it. The crews were real fancy, too, for each crummy had its Negro cook, who not only prepared the meals on the road but also kept the caboose clean and took care of the lanterns and markers. Those colored fellows were not on the railroad payroll but were paid by the crews. The company sanctioned their use. This practice died out before the Louisville & Nashville took over that line.

Conductor Southworth of the L&N, one of the many roads I worked for, was a notorious hater of hoboes. One bitterly cold night as his freight waited on a siding to meet another train his rear brakeman, Jim Jenkins, was making the usual inspection and found a Negro lad shivering on a flatcar loaded with lumber. The kid was nearly frozen. Having a wry sense of humor, Jim told him: "Boy, you'll freeze to death out here. You go back to the caboose and tell the brakeman there that the conductor said for you to get warm and ride the caboose."

The unsuspecting stowaway did so. Jim followed him a car-length behind, chuckling maliciously at the thought of the colored boy being thrown out bodily by a man who hated tramps. But when the Negro did not re-appear, Jim began to wonder what had happened. Later, he found out. The lad had timidly rapped on the caboose door and said the conductor had sent him. Southworth got wise instantly. He knew that the brakeman must have been playing a dirty trick on the kid. So he decided to turn the tables on Jim Jenkins.

"Are you hungry, boy?" he asked.

"Yes, sir," was the reply. "I ain't had a bite to eat since yesterday."

The conductor smiled. He knew that Jim's wife had packed a big lunch for the rear brakeman and now he, Southworth, would donate it to charity. Didn't the Bible say something about feeding the hungry?

"I've got some food here," he said pleasantly, "but my stomach's been botherin' me so I don't want it. You sit down at the table, boy, and eat all you can."

With that he placed the brakeman's well-filled lunch pail before the lad. Shortly afterward, Jim Jenkins entered the caboose in time to see the last of his edibles disappearing into the mouth of the stowaway. And what did Jim say about it? Not one damn word! Years later, however, he enjoyed telling the story on himself.

Our final caboose-meal story also comes from the South. The scene was Langtry, Texas, named for the beautiful actress Lillie Langtry, on the Southern Pacific main stem near the Pecos River Canyon. It was here that the famed Judge Roy Bean held his primitive court, "the only law west of the Pecos." His Honor also had an imbibing emporium that railroad men often patronized. That, of course, was before railroad managements adopted Rule G.

One day at noon a freight train pulled into Langtry. Trainmaster Murphy, who was riding the caboose, armed with a .44 Smith & Wesson, got off and walked up ahead to see the engineer about something, inadvertently leaving his revolver on the table. The rear brakeman had just cooked Mulligan stew for dinner. It was still simmering on the stove, ready to serve.

"Before we eat," the conductor said genially, "let's go over to Roy's place and hist one."

The suggestion fell on receptive ears. It being a hot sultry day, all hands were thirsty. After making sure the pot of Mulligan would not burn in their absence, the crew piled out of the crummy. Each man bought a round of drinks at Judge Bean's bar. Several minutes later the railroaders, with appetites sharpened by liquor,

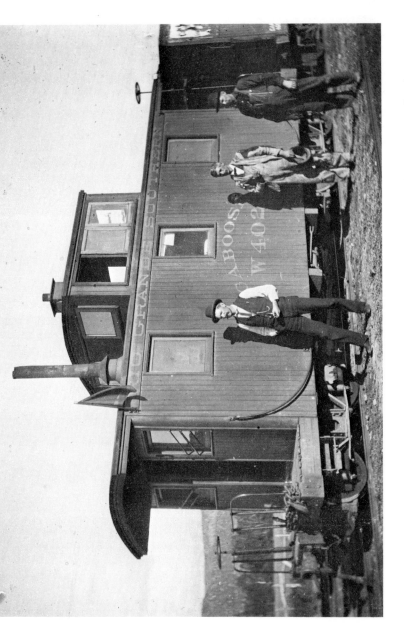

Once this Rio Grande Southern narrow gauge caboose rolled over the historic right-of-way up Lizard Head and Dallas Divide during Colorado's lusty youth.—DARRELL BREWER

returned to the caboose to eat dinner.

But during their absence, parties unknown had beaten them to it, like the three bears coming home after Goldilocks had eaten the baby bear's porridge. Bitter words followed. The crew angrily searched the train. They found three tramps hiding in an empty boxcar and charged them with the offense. The culprits admitted having devoured the stew, saying they were starved, and, in addition, having taken the trainmaster's revolver. They showed where the gun was hidden. Their only reason for stealing it, they said, was the fear that they might be shot for eating the meal.

By that time the crew had cooled off somewhat but decided to teach the hoboes a lesson. They led the trio to Judge Bean's front porch. The judge solemnly donned the symbol of his office, a battered top hat. After hearing the charge and listening to what the prisoners had to say, he sentenced two of them to three hours of hard work cleaning and scouring the caboose. The third 'bo, because he had made fun of the judge's hat, was doomed to "hang by the neck until dead," and at once.

A local merchant named Dodd, who doubled as an undertaker, put on a long-tailed black coat, turned his collar to simulate a preacher, and prayed long and fervently for "this poor soul who is about to appear before the Heavenly gates." A conveniently-located thick rope with a hangman's noose at one end was found and placed around the neck of the trembling prisoner. The other end was thrown over a heavy beam lashed to the caboose running board. For an instant Dodd tugged at the rope. Then he suddenly lifted it off the badly frightened tramp and said, "Now run like hell!"

I don't need to tell you how fast that guy picked 'em up and laid 'em down. The other two 'boes, who had been sentenced to clean the waycar, made such a good job of it that the skipper took them to the foreman of a Southern Pacific section gang and persuaded him to hire them. Stranger than fiction: two hoboes getting jobs as a by-product of caboose cookery.

This Chicago & Illinois Midland caboose puts a period to a long coal drag through Petersburg, Illinois, framed by a cornstalk that has long been the symbol of American abundance.—PHIL HASTINGS

FOUR

Beasts And Birds Ride The Caboose

A MILLION stars peppered the warm Arizona night. Our 60-car freight was too heavy for an old Mikado type to lug up the steep grade on one trip, so we stopped at Flowing Wells, a deserted hamlet, to cut our train in two and "double the hill." Months before, a Southern Pacific section gang had been stationed there but now the frame buildings were empty, warped, and sun-blackened. When the Mike returned to take the second half of our train up the grade conductor O. I. Lockwood lifted his oilburning lantern in a highball and swung aboard the caboose. As he opened the door a low growl and flashing white teeth startled him. He saw a small black and tan animal crouching on one of the bunks.

"Damned if it ain't a dog! Here, boy," he coaxed. "Come on, boy!"

He held out the back of one hand for the dog to sniff. The dog approached warily, satisfied himself that the offer of friendship was genuine, wagged his tail, and soon was jumping all over the man. When I caught the caboose at Iris he lay sprawled on the floor at the conductor's feet. He greeted me with wagging tail but did not leave "Lock."

We wondered where he had come from. The nearest habitation was Niland, several miles west, and we did not see how any creature except a lizard or a rattlesnake could have survived long at Flowing Wells which, despite its name, was waterless, its lone well having dried up even before the trackmen left. We fed him, of course—I have never known a railroad man to refuse to share his lunch with a hungry dog or cat—and Lock named him Boomer.

Well, sir, Boomer adopted that waycar as his home. He rode with us to Yuma and stayed in the caboose after that, traveling back and forth. At last, one morning my wife found his little body on the Indio station platform, waiting for a train that for him never came. We never knew what he died of nor, for that matter, how he'd ever got to Flowing Wells that starlit night.

Boomer and Hobo are fairly common names for train-riding dogs. The Chesapeake & Ohio boasts a Hobo, part chow and part shepherd, who at this writing has been riding freight trains in the caboose or diesel locomotive cab for the past ten years. Hobo has many railfaring friends. Come meal time, he is sure of a handout from at least one of them. His metal tag identifies him as belonging to someone in Richmond, Virginia, but he seems to be most at home when he hears "that lonesome whistle blowing across the trestle."

Hobo's first known train ride, as a puppy, was on a local freight into Lynchburg, the home city of C&O conductor R. T. Manley. The dog invited himself into Manley's caboose and was not driven out. That started his long series of unexplained journeys. Unlike most raildogs, Hobo gave his allegiance to the railway as a whole and not to any one employee. He is rightly named. His "inspection" trips take him over much of the C&O system, both the main stem and branch lines. He may be looking for someone or may just like to ride trains.

Another canine story comes to mind. Al Beers, a Missouri Pacific conductor, was running local freight out of Hoisington, Kansas. Shortly before they reached Hargrove one morning he leaned out the rear window of his crummy to look at the side of the train, and the case containing his eyeglasses fell from his pocket onto the "lone prairee."

"Pull the air, Jack!" he yelled excitedly to the rear brakeman, and Jack yanked the emergency cord. "I just lost my glasses," Al explained as the train slowed down. "I've got my eye on the spot where they fell but I'd have lost it if I came inside to pull the air myself."

The train stopped in a rural area about a mile from that spot. Al got off and walked back. As he was picking up the glasses he heard a faint whimper and glanced toward the right-of-way fence. A little spaniel had caught a paw in the twisted barbed wire. The conductor ran over to the suffering dog.

"Hold still and I'll get you loose," he said.

After freeing the animal, Al saw she was not only gaunt from pain, starvation, and exposure but was almost ready to give birth to pups. He carried her in his arms back to the crummy. His cupboard was well stocked. Al and Jack revived the spaniel with milk. They found a box, lined it with cotton waste, and lifted her into it. She ate often but only a little at a time until she regained her strength. Realizing that she must be a valuable dog, Al Beers spent several dollars advertising her in local newspapers, but to no avail.

A few days passed. One afternoon, after completing their station work, the two crew men returned to their caboose to find their pet nursing a litter of eight handsome puppies. As the latter grew old enough to be weaned, the conductor sold them, one after another, for ten dollars each. Their mother, if still living, is today a loved member of the Beers household in Hoisington.

Although the collie-shepherd named Rex has never ridden in a caboose, so far as I know, he belongs in this chapter because his base of operations is a Maine Central waycar. Every day for a dozen years or more, at this writing, Rex has been delivering newspapers to his master on an isolated farm in Maine near Curtis Corner on the Rumford branch. The conscientious critter, now an old friend of the crew, meets the local freight, which slows down while "Hank" Harradon, the conductor, crouching on the caboose steps, hands Rex one or two second-hand newspapers. The dog then takes them home to Ernest L. Buffum. It all started one day when Rex was a pup. He and Buffum were seated on the front porch of their trackside farmhouse watching a freight train go by. Then, for the first time, one of the crew men tossed off a rolled-up newspaper.

"Go fetch it!" ordered Buffum.

In a flash the collie-shepherd ran over to the track, picked up the paper with his jaws and proudly bore it to his master. From what I hear, he's been doing it on his own ever since, without once tearing a page—even when he knows there's a dog biscuit or some other goodie from a railroader's lunch pail tucked inside.

Many years ago R. H. Jenkins was a flagman in a Central of Georgia freight pool with F. H. Magruder, a conductor who liked to play pranks on his fellow crew members. One dark rainy night their train left Birmingham and stopped about a mile east of Oak Mountain Tunnel, with the caboose near the tiny depot of Vandiver, Alabama, in a wooded area infested with mountain lions and wild dogs.

"We're on the mountain side," the skipper told Jenkins. "Go back to the mouth of the tunnel and flag."

The flagman left reluctantly. He stayed out there in the rainy darkness for an hour and a quarter. "Everything looked spooky," he reported later. The locale reminded him of tales he'd heard of predatory beasts roaming thereabouts and he was greatly relieved when four long blasts of the engine whistle called him back to the train. As he opened the caboose door, still thinking of wild beasts, a creature standing unexpectedly on the toolbox greeted him with a prolonged *baa-a-a!* Terrified, he rushed out to the rear platform, only to hear his conductor laugh. The "wild beast" in the caboose proved to be a harmless young billygoat that Magruder had picked up at Vandiver.

It is commonplace when trains stop in forests during the winter for trainmen to feed hungry deer, squirrels, chipmunks, and other wildlife from their caboose steps and for such creatures to follow them into the crummy for more nourishment. One day a Canadian Pacific way freight running between London and Windsor, Ontario, halted suddenly in the wilderness near St. Joachim because engineer Cliff Knox did not want to run over a baby rabbit that stood on the track. The rear brakeman picked up the bunny and toted him into the van, as CPR cabooses are called; and the old skipper, Angus R. McDonald, nicknamed the critter "Sandy."

Sandy lived in that car for four years, riding about 100,000 miles, as undoubtedly the world's most-traveled rabbit. His favorite spot was on the conductor's desk. Whenever the engineer "whistled off," Sandy would brace his feet and lift his long ears to their full height, evidently aware that a jolt was coming. The doors on the caboose and the attached baggage car were never closed in front of him. One March day, shortly after Sandy had been adopted, McDonald decided that since spring had come the cottontail might like to run wild again and he put

Canadian Pacific conductor A. R. Mc-Donald and the rabbit named "Sandy" that lived in his van for four years and rode about 100,000 miles.

the little animal down on the snow-covered grass near St. Joachim. But when the whistle blew and the train started to move, instead of darting off into the woods, Sandy made rapid tracks toward the warm car. McDonald stopped the train and took long-ears on board again. Since that day, the crew men said, Sandy never left the train for as long as McDonald was operating it—except occasionally to be photographed.

Bunny was fed bananas, fruit cake, raisin cookies, grass, and plantain leaves and he had clean habits, using a sandbox provided for him in the baggage car. He showed an unwavering affection for McDonald and seemed to resent strangers. At length, when the old skipper took his pension Sandy disappeared. Maybe he answered the long-dormant call of the wild.

Another woodland creature, a fat groundhog, was leisurely crossing the Louisville & Nashville track behind a freight train parked on a siding near Stanford, Kentucky. Flagman George Durham spied it, caught the slow-moving animal, and tossed it into the back door of conductor John Pike's caboose, which was then passing his own. The flustered little beast kicked up a rumpus. Pike and his parlor brakeman, seated in the cupola together, decided that the invisible intruder was probably a wild bear. As their train began slowing down for a telegraph office on which they saw a red order board, Pike became uneasy. He realized that his duty was to get down from the doghouse, walk through the caboose past the obstreperous animal, whatever it was, and grab the order hoop that the operator would hold up to him as the train rolled by.

But he hedged. "You'd better get that order," he told the flagman.

"Not me," said Roy Owen. "You get it."

Instead of going out the usual way, the conductor crawled warily through the cupola window, walked along the waycar roof, and climbed down to the front platform just in time to seize the outstretched hoop, take off the flimsy, and toss the lightweight hoop back to the telegrapher. Then he peered through the window at the creature that had caused him so much trouble. Seeing what it was, he made up his mind that the crew would enjoy a well-seasoned groundhog stew that very night. And so they did.

I have never known a cat to ride a caboose except briefly. One day on the Southern Pacific, when I delivered a train order to my engineer I told him to take it easy so I could board the crummy. The train rumbled past me at a slow gait. Just before the caboose came I saw a big gray cat dart across the track and leap into the "possum belly." Now, the possum belly was a sort of locker, located on the under side of the waycar, in which we kept car chains, rerailing frogs, and buckets of "dope," or greasy waste used to repack hot journals. Its sliding doors had been warped by rain and were very hard to close. They left an opening about six inches wide, which the cat entered.

Well, I caught the caboose and discussed the cat with my rear brakeman, Frank Lillie. We thought there might be a litter of kittens in the possum belly. Sure enough, when we investigated at the next stop and peered into the dark opening we saw glistening yellow spots that said plainly "cats' eyes." Before we got going again, Frank rushed into the caboose, punched holes in a can of evaporated milk, and poured the milk into a shallow pan which he placed in the possum belly. Then we pulled out of town, and the cat and kittens were still there hours later when we tied up for the night. But next morning when we looked, they were gone. We never knew where they went, but it is possible that some sneaky coyote made a meal of them.

An Eastern conductor, who doesn't want his name mentioned, was operating a coal train one day when he entered his caboose to find a woman, a total stranger, seated on a locker. She was hugging a large white cat to her bosom and her breath smelled of liquor. According to her story, she quarreled with a coal-barge captain with whom she had been traveling from New York, ran away from the barge, and sought refuge in the nearby caboose.

"I was puzzled about what to do with her," my informant said. "I couldn't throw her off the train, but if any company official had seen her I might have been fired. So I phoned the railroad police at our next stop. Later, when we stopped again, the woman wanted to borrow three dollars from me to pay her fare back to New York, but I didn't have it and she started walking down the track, still hugging the cat, and that's the last time I ever saw her."

The same conductor told me about another cat which had

jumped down onto his caboose roof from an overhead bridge. He took the animal inside, fed it, and decided to keep it as a pet. But the feline visitor climbed back onto the roof and clung there while the train was making at least 45 miles per hour. What finally happened to it he doesn't know.

Strangest of all caboose riders was an alligator. One afternoon long ago conductor George W. Hilleany was standing on the waycar platform of an Illinois Central work train ballasted with gravel. They had stopped about ten miles out of New Orleans when he heard a queer noise and saw a small alligator which he described as "acting as if it was lonely." Desiring to make a pet of the reptile, George and his flagman lassoed it with a length of bell-cord from the caboose locker and, after some difficulty, got it into the crummy. They took it to Chatawa, Mississippi, where the conductor lived, and he gave it the run of a nice pond partly surrounded by reeds and cat-tails, with plenty of fish to eat.

The only other four-legged caboose rider I know about was a mule. Many years ago, certain Chesapeake & Ohio crews would surreptitiously buy cheap commodities in the Kentucky hills and haul them to market on their train without paying freight. This was possible in an era of lax supervision and loose accounting methods. Came the day, though, when division superintendent Fox looked into the matter. That September afternoon he left Ashland, Kentucky, on train No. 23 and went to Lexington.

About dark of the same day second No. 95, a string of empty boxcars with a caboose, pulled by a ten-wheeler, also departed from Ashland en route to Lexington. Tied in the rear of an old 36-foot boxcar was a wiry little mule, joint property of the conductor, "Dad" Seaman, and his longtime flagman, Clint West. They had bought the mule in Ashland for $15, knowing that in a Lexington market it would bring at least $75. Moreover, in a big grain car just ahead four hoboes were riding—secure from molestation because they had helped to get the mule into the boxcar.

Right behind the caboose a helper engine was laboring hard up Corey Hill when suddenly, with a crash and a hiss, Clint's head banged against the window sill. The hogger and fireman, each with a torch, followed by Clint with a lantern, quickly got off the train to investigate. They found that the end of the 36-foot car next to the caboose had been lifted clear off its trucks. It was badly splintered and jammed up against the crummy, but somehow all wheels remained on the rails. From within the waycar the air fairly sizzled with wild yells and profanity.

The three crew men hurried to the rear of the caboose. The fireman cursed. The others were momentarily struck dumb. From the opposite end of the crummy a mule faced them, its long ears tensed and teeth bared. It was standing in the narrow aisle between the lengthy leather cushions. On the floor, hunkered up in a knot, was old "Dad" Seaman. Every time the conductor moved the mule would squeal faintly and kick forward with a hind foot, smacking Dad in the posterior. The beast was not close enough to put much force into the kick, but Dad could not get out on either side—there was no room.

"Crawl out between his front legs!" Clint yelled.

"I tried that and the son of a bitch bit me," Dad shouted back. "Somebody get an axe and knock him on the head!"

"Wait a minute," Clint advised, grabbing the fireman's torch. "I'll stick this under his nose and when he rears up you jump out."

The instant the old skipper got clear of the mule, he made a dive for the locker to get an axe, but Clint restrained him. They found that the damage was less than they had thought; and so, with equipment taken from the possum belly, they chained up the ancient wooden car and eased it back down the mountain side and into clear on a spur—all in about 30 minutes.

After the caboose had been shoved up and coupled to the big grain car, the crew got together in a huddle that included the four grinning hoboes to work out a strategy. The mule would ride where it was, in the crummy. They might have gotten away with that easily if the telegraph operator at Morehead hadn't seen the mule, with ears wagging, stick its head out a caboose window. This unique situation was brought to the attention of superintendent Fox and the general yardmaster, Dan Reagan, at Lexington. Just as the red sun was rising behind the hills and second 95 was pulling into the yard the two brass collars walked rapidly to the east end. From behind a cut of cars they watched the train of rattlers click over the switch and down into track 3.

"You stay here, Reagan," the super said softly to the GYM as the caboose stopped almost opposite the spot where the officials were hiding.

Without knocking, Fox pushed open the rear door of the crummy, stepped inside, and glanced around. "Dad" Season was seated at a little folding desk up front, making out time slips. At the rear, flagman Clint West was down on his knees, industriously cleaning and filling the marker lamps.

"Hu-uh," the super gasped, "where is that mule?"

Open-mouthed and wide-eyed, the picture of amazement, Dad asked: "Mule? What mule?"

He glanced from his visitor to the flagman and then back to Fox. The latter explained rather lamely that he'd heard a report of a mule riding in the caboose on second 95. The pained expression he saw in each honest old face was touching. That their superintendent should suspect them of such a thing seemed almost more then they could bear. So sincerely sorry did the two miscreants appear that the mortified official actually felt ashamed of himself. He backed out of the rear door and as he walked back to the spot where he had left the general yardmaster he was probably determining to find out who had started that ridiculous tale and discipline him.

But what did happen to the mule? Oh, yes. The four hoboes had ingeniously gotten it out of the caboose just before the train steamed into the C&O yard and at that very moment were leading it by a rope down the road to the home of flagman Clint West.

There are authentic records, too, of birds riding cabooses. One bright July day a golden eagle with a six-foot wing span flew through an open cupola window and landed in the lap of the startled rear brakeman, A. H. Fonda, on Denver & Rio Grande Western train 68 about eight miles west of Walsenburg, Colorado, in the wooded hills. The great bird kept beating its powerful wings until Fonda and his skipper, H. W. Timney, subdued it under a coat. The men then tied its feet with cord and sent a message ahead via train radio. When the freight pulled into Pueblo a representative of the Colorado State Game and Fish Commission took charge of the captive, which they released after the local zoo had treated it for a minor wing injury.

And from the Great Northern comes word of conductor

Fletcher's pet parrot. This bird, according to Fletcher, could screech louder than a locomotive whistle. It annoyed the parlor brakeman, Tom something-or-other, by imitating the conductor's voice now and then, calling out, "Oh, Tom!" For the first two or three times Tom was fooled. He'd climb down from the doghouse to see what the skipper wanted, only to learn the parrot had summoned him. "Some day," he vowed, "I'm gonna wring that goddam bird's neck," which didn't bother Fletcher at all because he knew that Tom thought as much of the feathered nuisance as he did.

On one occasion, when the train crew were asleep in the crummy, a new callboy was sent to call them for their next run. It being his first night on the job, the kid was timid. The yardmaster told him: "Don't knock on the door. Just walk in and call 'em." Well, the lad went to the caboose but had hardly put a foot inside the door when the parrot let out an unearthly shriek. The callboy fled in terror, didn't use the steps but jumped from the platform and hit the ground running. After that, whenever he had to call a man in that crummy he'd pound on the side with a rock. Thereupon the parrot would squawk; and that, with the thumping, woke up the crew.

Another parrot-lover, conductor Shaver on the Oklahoma & Northwestern, preferred the small species known as love-birds. He also had pet canaries. To get into Shaver's waycar was like barging into an aviary. There were cages to the right, cages to the left, cages in front, and a musical chorus of trills and chirps. I guess he had about 20 cages in that caboose, and this hobby brought him a tidy sum. Shaver bred and sold birds for years, using the proceeds to put his son through college.

Two stories about wildfowl will wind up this chapter. In the autumn of 1906, while the mallards were migrating southward, a Burlington freight train rattled and clanked its way through a dense fog. Brakeman Perry Mays, seated in the cupola, worried because the "pea soup" prevented observation of his train. Suddenly a solid object crashed against one of the cupola windows, breaking the glass, letting in a cold wind, and hitting his chest with a thump that knocked the air out of him. Instinctively he threw his arms around the object, clasping it tight. When he regained his breath he found himself holding a live wild duck!

The migrant, evidently separated from its flock by the fog, had flown too low and shattered the caboose window. Mays was startled but unhurt except for two small cuts from jagged glass. When he climbed down from the doghouse the duck was still stunned. It soon became alert and tried to escape. The brakeman, aided by his conductor, tied its feet and put it in an empty box. They observed that the tip of one wing had been severed by glass, making flight difficult if not impossible. In sympathy with its plight, the two railroaders gave the duck rice, which it quickly gobbled up. The next day they let the captive walk around the caboose floor but with one foot tied to the stove by a sizeable piece of cord. As that was the season for grain movement by rail, they easily got enough wheat from empty boxcars to feed their new mascot.

At first the crew spoke of the fine duck dinner they'd get, but the longer that mallard stayed with them the less they said about eating it. After a week or so the wild duck had become so tame that it would quack a greeting when one of them entered the waycar. But one day the bird was missing. What happened to it I don't know. Some other crew may have swiped it for a meal.

A strangely moving story from the Canadian National Railways tells of a wild goose that broke precedent by spending an entire winter in Nova Scotia instead of migrating to the South with its flock. A way-freight crew first noticed it around the time that goldenrod heralded the return of autumn. They saw the goose hovering over their van day after day, week after week. Flying low, it would settle down on the caboose roof, riding some distance and then winging aloft again but always keeping near the little car on its run from one terminal to another, even when the crew was making setouts and pickups. This puzzled the railway men. They knew that wild geese normally headed down into the States for the winter, but this one didn't. The goldenrod faded, autumn leaves withered, and biting cold winds, followed by snow, swept across Nova Scotia, but still the bird kept its lonely vigil.

The crew surmised that the goose had last seen its mate on the roof of their van and that the gander may have fallen under the wheels or, more likely, been shot by a hunter, and the survivor stuck around with the hope that the lost one would return.

Filled with pity, the men heaped little piles of grain and other food on the caboose roof, day after day, inside a small framed enclosure that they had built to keep it from blowing away, and the bird would eat it. Even when snow buried the countryside in a white silence, they kept a patch of the roof clear for the wild goose.

Somehow the solitary bird survived that cruel winter; and in the late spring, when northbound migrants again began flying into Nova Scotia, it disappeared. Ornithologists studying the case expressed the belief that it found another mate in the flock it had left the preceding fall.

Rear brakeman hangs up the marker lamps as a freight on the Texas
& Louisiana lines of Southern Pacific makes ready to leave Del Rio
for San Antonio.—SOUTHERN PACIFIC

FIVE

Marker Lights, Lanterns, and Fusees

ET'S LOOK at the equipment regularly carried in cabooses in the days before they were electrically lighted, some of which is still carried today. Take marker lights, for example. These play a major role; no train is complete without them. The rule books define *train* as "an engine or motor or more than one engine or motor coupled, with or without cars, displaying markers." Note the last two words.

The commonly accepted marker is cylindrically shaped and has four lenses: three green (a few roads use amber instead) and one red. They are hung as brackets on each side of the waycar projecting outward and thus visible to the head end of the train. That arrangement was adopted in the days before air-brakes. As long as the engineer, by looking back, could see that green light he knew his train was complete and not broken-in-two. The brackets are placed in such a way as to permit the rotation of markers when desired. While a train is running, the markers are turned to show red at the rear and green to the front and sides. When a train takes a siding, the markers are rotated to show green to the rear, front, and outside, the red being toward the center. The colors mean the same by day and night, although in daytime many green markers appear to be bluish green. Rules require that they be lighted from sunset to sunrise. Markers burn kerosene and are reasonably windproof and shockproof.

When I first went into train service we used a different kind of marker. It consisted of a box, with glass panes in front and back, built on the side of the cupola and containing a flat-bottomed lamp. By opening a tiny cupola door you could set the lamp in or take it out for cleaning and filling with oil, and change the two panes of glass, one red, the other white, placed according to which direction you are going. There was also an overhead light with a small hinged door swinging downward. You put your lamp and panes through that door. A spring catch held the glass in place. These catches were none too secure. After a number of brakemen had been sabred in the neck by panes that worked loose, overhead lamps were discontinued.

Forerunners of the modern electric hand lamp used for signals today have a long and varied history. Even non-railroaders are intrigued by the weaving, bobbing lanterns of night-train traffic. Lanterns are indispensable. When they are darkened, all night movements in yard and road transportation are halted.

Relatively few trainmen living today have handled, as I have, four different methods of lantern illumination. Sperm oil from whales came first, as it did for fixed signals also, but before my time. The lantern fuels I am familiar with were lard (usually with some sperm oil mixed in), signal oil, kerosene, and electricity. Lard oil had a low solidifying point, about two degrees below freezing, and would get as hard as a pawnbroker's heart. To offset that, a piece of copper wire shaped like a hairpin, or even a hairpin borrowed from a lady, was run through the burner with the ends of the wire pointing up. The points were bent inward so that the flames heated them, thus conveying heat downward into the oil. In winter you often had to thaw out your lantern on a redhot stove.

Next came the day of signal oil. This had some peculiar properties, but after you learned about them and used your lantern accordingly it couldn't be beaten. A wick burned too long lost its capillary attraction. Oil left in the fount too long became cloudy with white specks floating in it. So if you changed your wick twice a month, emptied its fount once in a while, and kept the crust scraped off the burner, you had efficient lighting.

94

Crisp morning cold holds the plumes of coal smoke as a Canadian Pacific steamer on mixed train No. 117, running between Brownville Jct., Maine, and Megantic, Quebec, Canada, rejoins its train.—PHIL HASTINGS

Then, for economical reasons, the railroads tried kerosene. What a flop that was, at first! Ten minutes after you lit your wick the globe was smoke-blackened. Jiggle your lantern a little and out would go the flame. After several months of experimenting, the companies supplied kerosene lanterns so drafted that they smoked less but never worked as well as those which used signal oil.

Finally we had electric lanterns. When they were first introduced, if an employee wanted one he bought it himself. The battery was supposed to burn continuously for 16 hours, but after one-quarter of that time the light began to dim and after eight hours you had to strike a match to see if your lantern was still burning! Inasmuch as a battery cost 65 cents, a fair-sized sum in those days, not much time passed before you discarded your wonderful electric gadget and went back to kerosene. Today, of course, the railroad furnishes its employes with both lanterns and batteries. The electric type weighs about four times as much as an oil lantern and, believe me, after you've lugged one of 'em around for eight hours on duty they get plenty heavy. The light is brilliant but does not spread as far as that of the oil lantern.

A few roads tried indicator lights, each one being a long sash framing five panes of white translucent glass. In each pane you would put a black stencil that denoted the train's number: X-259, or whatever it might be. A semi-circular metal box covered the sash and held the light. The shapes of hand lanterns used over the years showed a wide diversity, beginning with a square type with flat glass and protecting ribs patented by J. H. Rohman in 1857. Some conductors used two-toned lantern globes—red, green, or blue above and clear below—so that the engineer could distinguish them from the monotone lanterns carried by brakemen.

The earliest lantern globes I remember were very brittle; we seldom made a trip in those days without shattering one or two. A trainman signaling with his lantern is not always careful to hold it vertical as he should. If you tilted a brittle lantern globe so that the flame touched the glass—*bang!* A piece would fall out or the globe might break into many fragments. Later on, a tougher grade of glass was used.

Coming now to the flags carried in cabooses: the item in the book of rules I remember best is No. 99, "When a train stops

"All clear, let her go!" as a conductor swings the highball with his hand lantern. Forerunners of the modern electric hand lamp used for signals today have a long and varied history. In the scene above, a Southern Pacific conductor lights his red kerosene hand lantern.— H. L. KELSO *(Top — Right)* The familiar *Highball* with an electric hand lamp.—H. L. KELSO *(Right)* Brakeman signaling a freight train out of the yards. This method was replaced long ago by the radio-telephone and walkie-talkie.—SOUTHERN PACIFIC

Switchmen's lanterns wink beside them as they wait the return of the switcher at a New York Central yard.—JIM SHAUGHNESSY When electric lanterns were first introduced, an employee had to buy it himself. Today, most of America's railroads furnish both the lantern and the batteries. (Left) A Southern Pacific diesel helper reassembles the freight train after cutting out at Norden Summit, having helped extra 6311 East up the Sierra grade. Action takes place under the famous Donner Pass snow sheds. Note how the flash reflects off the snow flakes filtering through the shed.—PHIL HASTINGS

under circumstances in which it may be overtaken by a following train, flagman will at once proceed back a sufficient distance to insure full protection." The same rule also deals with stop signals, such as: In daylight the flagman ordinarily carried a red flag, two fusees, and at least three torpedoes, or "guns," and at night one white lantern, one red lantern, two fusees, and maybe three but often as many as a dozen torpedoes. Almost every caboose I was ever in had, over the end door, a tightly-rolled red flag with three torpedoes around it or had affixed to its staff a Bull Durham sack containing three torpedoes. The brakeman who picked it up was likely to have half a dozen more torpedoes in his coat pocket.

Torpedoes are audible signals, fusees visible signals. Both give you a mighty comfortable feeling when you are out flagging in a dense fog or a heavy snowstorm where, without them, an oncoming engineer might be right on top of you before he could see your red flag. Many years ago, a Broadway play called "Casey Jones" had a railroad man grab a red flag (but no lantern, fusee or torpedo) to flag a train at night. As you might guess, that play didn't last long.

The brakeman walks back to cover as flagman for his Michigan Division freight train on the New York Central. On the alert for trains which may be approaching from the rear, he is keenly aware of the importance of his task to the safety of his fellow railroaders and himself. The flagman always makes sure he has a supply of torpedoes and fusees in his pocket for use as emergency to other trains.—NEW YORK CENTRAL (*Left*) A brakeman is "short flagging" in this scene in the Feather River Canyon of the Western Pacific. The term "short flagging" means the brakeman is not far enough from his train to protect it from the rear.—DONALD DUKE

One night when I was braking freight on the Frisco Lines in Missouri, we stopped at the village of Sleeper. We had enough time to take coal and go on to the next station ahead of a fast passenger train. But the coal chute had gone haywire. The fireman could not raise it from the tender and we couldn't move without running the risk of tearing it off and perhaps dumping several tons of black diamonds onto the main line. Our train was standing in a pea-soup fog that restricted our vision to a car-length or two. I began worrying lest the streak of varnish would come up while we were still there. Then a long whistle blast followed by three short ones sent me back to protect the rear of our train.

As a rule, a flagman *walks* back, but this time I ran. I counted eight telegraph poles, laid a torpedo on the rail, stuck a fusee into the ground beside it to mark the spot, and continued running until I had counted eight more telegraph poles. Then I planted two more torpedoes and returned to the first potential noise-maker.

Soon I heard the blare of the passenger engine as she stormed through the mist at high speed. I pulled the bonnet off a fusee and got ready to light it. *Bang! bang!* sounded the two guns. The blare ceased abruptly but the whir of wheels rushing through the mark continued. When I saw the headlight I gave a "washout," a violent stop signal, with my lantern.

The brakes went into emergency with a screech of compressed air and the car wheels, gripped by the brakes, cast off sparks that looked like rings of fire. The engine ran by me a few car-lengths before she stopped. I told the hogger why I had flagged him. He pulled down, headed through a siding, and kept on going. Meanwhile, our conductor had called the section gang. They jacked the chute back into position and we, too, went on our way. I'll never forget hearing that welcome sound of torpedoes out there in the fog.

A torpedo looks much like a small tin pillbox with two lead strips attached. One strap bends around the rail head to protect the torpedo from being jarred off; the other is a sort of pigtail that lays along the rail. A wheel running onto this other strap keeps it in place. Like everything else, torpedoes have undergone many changes over the years. The first ones I remember were simply paper-wrapped explosives, the paper being dipped in tar. One day,

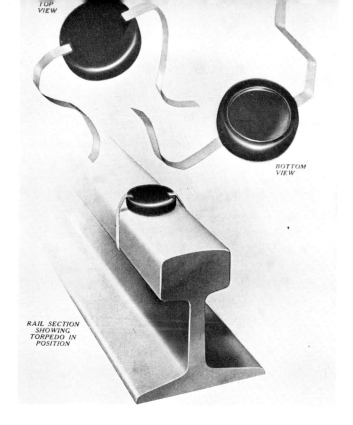

TOP
VIEW

BOTTOM
VIEW

RAIL SECTION
SHOWING
TORPEDO IN
POSITION

Every caboose in service carries a supply of torpedoes. Oldest make on the American market is the Schooley, first used in 1874, now made by Columbia Railway Signal Company. *(Below)* Torpedo manufactured by the Standard Railway Fusee Corp., one of many types attached to the rail to warn any oncoming train that another train is just ahead.

while I was separating a bunch of torpedoes that had become stuck together by the warm weather's effect on the tar, my conductor, Neighbor Little, told me his version of the origin of the railroad torpedo.

"During the Civil War," he said, "a Union soldier serving as a brakeman went back to flag in a storm. His lantern went out and he feared the engineer of an oncoming train would not see him, so he set his box of musket caps on a rail, plastering it in place with a handful of mud. Sure enough, the oncoming hogger ran by him, but the engine wheels broke the box of caps. The explosion and bright flash gave the engineer the impression that something on his eight-wheeler had broken, so he stopped as soon as he could; and that was the first recorded use of torpedoes in railroad operation."

The next type of torpedo that I worked with had been dipped in sealing wax to prevent heat from softening it. This device had a small hole in the center, through which you shoved a peg, much like a wooden shoepeg, between joints to secure it to the rail. Inasmuch as many rail-joints in those days were an inch or two wide, it was not dependable. Then came the tin pillbox, and some roads used a turtle-back type with steel springs instead of lead straps.

Using the tin pillbox was hazardous. More than a few trainmen were injured by the pieces of tin that flew in all directions when the torpedo exploded. The present type is fibre-covered. It is just as loud and a lot safer. Some unsung genius invented a four-tined little pitchfork for placing torpedoes on the track from the rear of a caboose in motion and holding them there until they exploded. It worked fairly well until the weight of rail exceeded 75 pounds per yard. Modern rail weighing nearly twice that much has too large a head for the torpedo fork.

And now I will draw a word-picture of another signal appliance that the caboose carries. Let's say you are a flagman on the Frisco in the old days. Your conductor is worried by the train's slow speed. "We're gonna have that varnish on our tail if we keep draggin' along like this," he tells you. "In about two minutes you'd better drop off a yellow one."

A yellow fusee, of course. You climb down from the cupola and go to that familiar red metal cabinet fastened to the wall. This

New Haven brakeman takes a yellow fusee from the rack of his caboose.

 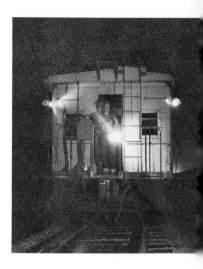

Trainmaster's clerk displays two types of fusees, red and yellow, giving you an idea of their size.—CHICAGO & NORTH WESTERN *(Top—Right)* A Union Pacific trainman prepares to ignite a fusee.—UNION PACIFIC *(Below)* When a fusee tossed from the rear platform of a caboose sticks upright in a tie it's probably good luck rather than good marksmanship. But no matter where they land, they'll burn bright.—CANADIAN PACIFIC

cabinet is about 30 inches high, 20-wide, and 6-deep, with two small sliding doors near the bottom. One door is labeled "Matches" and the other "Torpedoes." You lift the top of the cabinet. A hinged flap falls forward, revealing some paper cylinders that resemble the species of fireworks known as Roman candles. Most of them are red; the rest are a bright yellow.

You draw out one of the yellow cylinders, seize the loose end of a piece of friction tape stuck across the cap's head, and tear it loose. Under the tape is affixed a quantity of black stuff like that on boxes of safety matches. One end of the cylinder in your hands has a sharp spike projecting (today these spikes are no longer used) while the opposite end is slightly larger than the main part. This enlarged part is the cap or bonnet. You grasp the fusee's center with one hand and its cap with the other, and remove the cap.

Now your entire fusee has the same diameter, one and one-eighth inches, from end to end, but the igniting end has some of the stuff your safety matches have. You step out on the rear platform of the crummy, point the fusee away from you, and draw

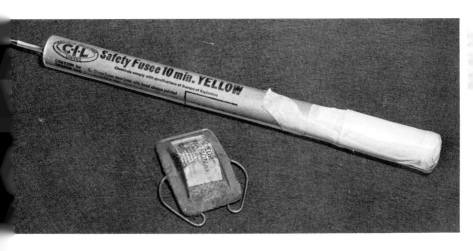

Strontium nitrate makes a fusee burn red; sodium makes it burn yellow. In the foreground a torpedo with clamps.—CANADIAN PACIFIC RAILWAY

107

the end of the cap across the fusee's head. Sparks fly, a tiny blue flame shows, and then a brilliant yellow light hisses out.

You hold the fusee a few seconds to be sure it is well ignited. Then you lean over the rear platform and drop the fusee, with its spike slanted toward the engine, and have the satisfaction of seeing it strike a tie and burn in a more or less upright position. "Hot dog!" you chuckle. "Right on the nose!" There's about one chance in 50 of your fusee sticking upright in a tie when dropped, and when it does land that way it's due more to luck than to skill. Let's say rain is falling heavily. But as you look back to where you dropped the fusee you see a vivid yellow glare undimmed by the downpour. You wonder what your grandfather would have thought of that!

I was looking at an antique book of rule issued June 13, 1858, by the single-tracked Atlantic, Gulf & West Indies Terminal Railroad (now part of Seaboard Air Line). Rule 13 defined the procedure to be followed in the days before fusees:

> Should a train run off, or for any reason be stopped on the track at night, the red light must be instantly sent back to a safe distance to stop a train approaching from the rear, and the green light will in like manner be sent forward to stop a train approaching the front, and at that point a fire must be built in the middle of the track, and a train hand stationed there who shall keep the fire and the green light burning.

Even early in the present century, terms like "train hand," "car hand," and "track hand" were commonly used. I remember a Frisco conductor making a demonstration for his train hand, meaning me, at a time when every Frisco caboose carried a wood barrel kept full of water. Taking a red fusee from the rack, he lit it, waited a few seconds for it to burn, and then dropped it upright into the water barrel. The spike stuck in the wooden bottom and the fusee continued to burn for the entire ten minutes it was supposed to stay lit.

But not even a rain-burning fusee can guarantee your train's safety. Behind its yellow a whiter light may be shining, still far off but quickly growing stronger—the electric headlight of an oncoming express. Your own train must get into the clear before it arrives. Slack runs in with a bump; your engine is near the switch now and is slowly heading in. It'll be close, you reflect, maybe too damn close. You grab your red lamp and two red fusees sticking up in the floor, ready for action if necessary. Suppose your train were to break in two? If that should happen, you'd sure have to pick 'em up and lay 'em down fast. You poke your head around a corner of the crummy to see how close the switch is and then you look at the fast-approaching headlight.

Now your caboose is but a few car-lengths from the switchstand. The "varnish" swings around the curve behind you and shines brightly on your face. You light a red fusee and stick it in the rear platform, knowing its crimson glare is many times stronger than your marker lights and the passenger hogger can't fail to see it. You don't want to stop or delay him, of course, as you would do if you were to drop a red fusee from your train. "A fusee burning red on or near the track," says the standard book of rules, "must not be passed until burned out."

As your caboose pulls into the siding curve you call out to the conductor: "Oh, Cap, grab this torch, will ya, and put it in the stove." The skipper dashes out, glances to see if his car is by the fouling point, twists the markers until they show green, and then jerks the red fusee loose and carries it inside. You swing a highball. The oncoming engine gives a bellowing roar in salute as the hogger widens on his throttle again. You walk after your own train from the switch you have just cleared, thinking, "Doggone if a fusee ain't handy to have around when you need it!"

But no device is foolproof. Misuse a fusee and you might cause trouble. Now and then careless trainmen deliberately remove the caps from fusees, exposing the friction ends, so as to have them ready for instant use. Such blunders have set more than one caboose afire. Sometimes the wooden racks which hold the supply of fusees have holes too small to slip the fusees through, thus inadvertently pulling off the caps. Another hazard is to leave fusees, torpedoes, nails, scrap-iron, and other junk mixed together in a box.

Three or four Midwestern roads use green fusees in hand signaling. These fusees are made with either wooden or paper handles and burn five minutes. In the previous century, when the caution signal was green and the clear indication white, the Santa Fe, Chicago & Alton, and maybe a few other roads used a 15-minute fusee that burned red for the first five minutes, green for the next five, and then white for five minutes.

The burnable part of red fusees consist of 70 per cent strontium nitrate, 14 per cent sulphur, 10 per cent potassium perchlorate, 4 per cent sawdust, and 2 per cent oil. Most of the strontium nitrate in yellow fusees is supplanted by barium or sodium nitrate while in green fusees, which are rather rare, barium nitrate replaces the strontium entirely.

Fusee requirements are strict. Each fusee must be able to support a weight of 120 pounds at the halfway mark between two points four inches apart. Eighty per cent of the fusees tested by manufacturers must remain burning after being dropped 30-feet onto a hard surface. The ignition compound must be waterproof so it will ignite by the usual means even after being soaked in water ten minutes. A fusee, after burning ten seconds in air, must be able to burn not less than ten minutes when submerged in a vertical position with head down. These are but a few of the many technical tests and requirements for the manufacture of fusees.

Employes' timetables of the Pennsylvania Railroad state that a cabin car—the Pennsy's term for caboose—should carry 12 fusees, more in times of bad weather. A certain PRR conductor on an Indiana run apparently was very pessimistic about the weather. Whenever he went out on a run he took extra fusees, without checking on how many he already had. A surprise inspection of his supplies revealed 288 fusees, enough for 24 cabin cars!

"And that wasn't all," lamented stores inspector James J. Walsh. "The cabin also had 72 torpedoes, three times as many as his timetable called for. Also four extra cushions, six extra air hoses, and nine globes for hand lanterns. In all, $130 worth of supplies that shouldn't have been there. Such hoarding is a real headache. It means we have to buy more materials than we actually need. It means dribbling away money we could use in a lot better ways."

That particular tour by Walsh was, he said, "an eye-opener." Looking into more than 200 cabin cars, he found that one out of three had excess supplies. One contained 24 hand lanterns, most of

110

which would have gone out-of-date before the crew could ever use them. Another cabin yielded 11 air hoses, another had four extra brooms, and in still another he discovered 300 torpedoes.

Fusees cost the Pennsy hundreds of thousands of dollars a year. Overstocking is wasteful because a fusee is supposed to be used within nine months of the date stamped on the wrapping. After that, it may sputter when lit—even explode. Also increasing the bill for fusees are many carelessly stored, becoming wet and useless; fusees used instead of matches to start trash fires; and those taken off railroad property for 4th of July celebrations, for highway flares for the family auto, and for making campfires.

Walsh started his tour of the system by taking a five-mile walk through a yard, scattered along the tracks of which he found six marker lights, four flagmen's cases, and 12 hand lanterns, with a total value at that time of $191.48 going to waste. Said he: "The trainmen could help a lot by checking their supplies, returning any excess, and in future taking only what they need for a trip."

I don't know who invented the fusee or the railroad torpedo, but much of the credit for those cabooses accessories should go to the ancient Chinese who developed fireworks.

Under the light of hand lanterns, a Pittsburg & Shawmut Railroad crew check the train list —familiar sight on any railroad.—R. J. COOK

Public school children visit the old caboose at Oneonta, New York, in which the Brotherhood of Railroad Trainmen was founded in 1883.

SIX

Cabooses That Made History

ENSHRINED in a quiet park at Oneonta, New York, apart from other railroad equipment is Delaware & Hudson caboose No. 10. This red, wooden-bodied four-wheeler no longer winds its way through the wooded Catskill Mountains, swaying and chain-clanking, but stands immobilized as a relic of the "good old days" that weren't so good after all, and the beginning of a movement designed to make them better. It takes us back nearly a century.

During the first five years of readjustment after the Civil War, when railroading was so hazardous that no trainman could get insurance, seven out of ten of America's train-crew members were killed or seriously injured on the job, according to figures from Cleveland national headquarters of the Brotherhood of Railroad Trainmen. A cartoon of that period showed an applicant for a job as brakeman being told there was no opening at that time but to return next Thursday, when it was likely that a man would have been killed.

In those days there was no workmen's compensation, social security, unemployment insurance, minimum wage, or medicare, not even an eight-hour day. For many of us as late as the 1890's, when I went braking for the Southern Pacific, a seven-day week on the railroad was not uncommon. Organized labor was then in its infancy. Ruthless methods were used to break strikes, and strikers were blackballed. Workers had no legal redress from injury or death due to employers' negligence.

Against this grim background the BRT was founded September 13, 1883, by eight determined men who met in caboose No. 10, parked in the Delaware & Hudson freight yard at Oneonta. This car was assigned to conductor Charles J. Woodworth. With him in that historic session were William Gurney, Daniel Hopkins, Elmer Wessel, H. S. Wilbur, Daniel J. and Eugene McCarty, and Union C. Osterhout, all employed in train or yard service on the Susquehanna Division. Wessel summed up the group's moderate objectives by saying: "We want better working conditions and some kind of insurance for those who might be stricken by illness, injury, or death."

Calling themselves the Brotherhood of Railroad Brakemen, these eight men chose Woodworth as their first grand master. The move spread rapidly; local lodges sprang up all over the country. In 1889 the organization adopted its present name, Brotherhood of Railroad Trainmen. Today the BRT, with some 200,000 members including myself, is the largest of all rail operating unions.

In 1924 the Delaware & Hudson, at its own cost, restored No. 10 to its original condition, using couplers and trucks from another caboose, attached memorial plaques to its sides, and installed it in the Oneonta park. Inside is a small, black, cylindrical stove, not the more common pot-bellied type but with the usual smokestack jutting out of the car roof. The oversize tray atop it is big enough to hold cooking utensils and is surrounded by a flange or collar to keep them from being jogged off by the train's motion. High above it, suspended from the ceiling, is a gigantic spool. This spool was used for winding up a long thick cord which extended over the car tops at night to connect with a bell in the engine cab for communicating with the hogger.

Old No. 10 is partly sheltered from bad weather by a red, sloping, fluted-tile roof supported by a four-sided white column at each corner and is visited by many tourists, especially railroaders and railfans. At the 1966 convention of the National Model Rail

Exterior and interior view of the old caboose where the Brotherhood of Railroad Trainmen was organized. In the view below, the overhead spool was used for winding up a long cord which, at night, extended over the tops of the cars and connected with a bell in the engine cab.

THIS CABOOSE WAS LOANED LIEUTENANT PEARY BY THE ERIE RAILROAD AND WENT ON HIS EXPEDITION IN 1899; WAS USED AS DECKHOUSE ON SHIP WINDWARD AND AS SLEEPING QUARTERS AT ETAH. ITS HIGHEST LATITUDE WAS 70° NORTH, AND IT IS THE ONLY RAILROAD CAR EVER SENT TO THE ARCTIC REGIONS.

ERIE RAILROAD

4259

This caboose was loaned to Peary by the Erie Railroad and went on his famous arctic expedition in 1899. This is the only railroad car ever sent to the arctic regions.—ERIE-LACKAWANNA ARCHIVES

road Association the BRT awarded $1,300 in prizes for the five most exact miniature replicas of this caboose. The average amount of time that each entrant spent on his model was 1,000 hours. In one of the two first-prize models, the work of Frank De Santis, it is possible to build a wood fire in the tiny stove and to slam the door shut—the door-knob and latch as well as brakes, marker lanterns, etc., are fully working. The second-prize model, by Louis Curry, although only about three inches long, is held together with hand-made, scale-sized nuts and bolts, and the names on the original's plaques are reduced to scale and readable under a magnifying glass!

As I have stated, *caboose* was originally a nautical word for "little house on a ship's deck." The only railroad waycar fitting this description was an Erie four-wheeler, No. 4259, built at the company's shops in 1892 with a rounded roof but no cupola, and used on short runs. Growing freight tonnage soon made this type obsolete. When the 4259 was six years old a smashup lifted its small wooden body right off the trucks. A wrecking crew loaded the wreckage onto a flatcat, hauled it to Susquehanna, Pennsylvania, and left it in the yard for scrapping. Captain Robert E. Peary, U.S.N., saw the caboose body while he was visiting a lifelong friend, president E. B. Thomas of the Erie, and observed that it was solidly built and snug. Except for the truck being sheared off, it had survived the wreck undamaged.

"I could use that thing on my next expedition," the Arctic explorer said in effect, "for winter headquarters in Greenland."

Thomas said the railroad would gladly loan it to him for as long as he needed it. So the "de-horned" vehicle was loaded onto a flatcar again and this time was taken to New York City, where on July 4, 1898, it was hoisted onto the main deck of Peary's steamship *Windward* and bolted down to keep heavy seas from sweeping it overboard. A week later, with immense throngs crowding the docks to wave good-bye, the *Windward* lifted anchor for an exciting voyage to the Far North.

Years afterward, the explorer's daughter, Marie A. Peary, wrote a book for children entitled *North Pole Caboose*, based on her father's writings and her own trip to Greenland with him, in which she stated: "Many strange experiences were in store for the caboose. The air became colder every day, and soon in the blue water around the ship great lumps of ice began to appear. The days were growing longer, too, until there was scarcely any night at all, just gray twilight, and then suddenly the sun would be shining again."

While at sea the 4259 served as a deckhouse. During that first winter of howling gales and ice blocking his ship for eight dark months in Allmay Bay, Grinnell Land, the explorer used the caboose as his headquarters and living room but actually slept away from it more nights than he spent aboard ship. Then in August 1889, the party set up a base of operations at Etah, Greenland, high up on a white cliff where no snow, rocks or ice could tumble down from overhead. Eskimos helped the white men to get the "little house" ashore and up the cliff with heavy ropes wrapped around it and tied at each end to stakes driven deep in the ground.

"Then the unloading of the ship began," Miss Peary wrote. "The Commander was going to stay in Greenland a year or more to explore the country. He put Eskimos to work bringing up the boxes of provisions. These were all exactly the same size and were used to build a wall around the caboose, about six feet high and about two feet away from it on all sides. It was just as if the caboose were enclosed in a six-foot fence made of boxes. When the wall was finished, canvas was spread from the top of the wall to the caboose roof and held firmly in place by heavy stones."

Later, snow was heaped against the box wall on all sides and over the canvas, turning the hack into an igloo, warm and snug for the winter. Deer and musk-ox skins hung outside and laid on the floor added to the coziness. Outside, the winter was very long, dark, and bitterly cold, but indoors were warmth from a coal stove, light from oil lamps, food a-plenty, and time for writing, reading, and getting their equipment into the best possible condition. Now and then curious Eskimo children visited the caboose, and hunting parties supplied fresh meat.

In 1900, when spring brought sunlight and higher temperatures, Peary and his men made a spectacular exploration of northern Greenland. The caboose remained untenanted at Etah until the

118

The caboose Peary took to the Arctic as it looked on exhibition at
Susquehanna, Pennsylvania, shortly before fire destroyed it in 1940.
—ERIE-LACKAWANNA ARCHIVES

Windward returned to pick it up after a second ice-locked winter,
1900-1901, spent at Fayer Harbor near Cape Sabine on Grinnell
Land. The waycar was then hoisted aboard ship again. At length,
in July 1902, Peary gave it back to the Erie Railroad at New-
burgh, New York. Thus a piece of railroad equipment had given
four years of service to an Arctic expedition but never reached the
North Pole, although it did go as far north as 70 degrees of latitude.

After that, the 4259 was stored at Shohola, New York. Then
came the glorious news that on April 6, 1909, Peary had reached
the North Pole, which no white man before had ever seen. Aware
of the publicity value involved, Erie officials had the 4259 rebuilt
at their Buffalo Shops and sent on a triumphal tour of the entire
system. Finally the wheels were removed again and the old seago-
ing caboose was exhibited at Susquehanna until a fire of undeter-
mined origin reduced it to charcoal in 1940. It had its day of glory.

The fighting of World War I ended with an Armistice pact signed in a railroad passenger car parked in a French forest. Many years afterward, Adolf Hitler dictated terms for a capitulation of the French Army in that same car. These facts are well known. But relatively few people know that in 1911 a Mexican insurrection ended with a surrender on board a caboose of the San Diego & Arizona, a railway then in course of construction.

This insurrection was a bloody attempt by the International Workers of the World, known as "Wobblies," to take the Mexican town of Tijuana in Baja California by force of arms and establish their own government there. It greatly annoyed sugar king J. D. Spreckels in his efforts to build the "impossible" railway through Carriso Gorge. The rebels' first leader, "General" Price, declared: "Spreckels has millions and large interests in this area. We aim to make him and other large holders contribute heavily to the support of our army."

On May 8th the Wobblies began hostilities by cutting telegraph wires along the rail line to distract attention from their projected attack on Tijuana. The following day they killed the mayor of Tijuana, burned the town's church and bull ring, and chased many residents across the border into the United States. Then Price put guards on the construction trains to ensure the railroaders' neutrality. Posing as a *de facto* government, his men requisitioned railway supplies from the trains, giving worthless receipts for them.

On May 19th they raided the construction workers' camp and seized a train operated by conductor W. G. McCormick; but the skipper, with a glib tongue, persuaded them to leave, after which he took his train safely back to San Diego. On May 24th Price arrested some railway laborers and jailed them overnight in Tijuana, but McCormick, again by fast talking, got them out in the morning.

Five days later the rebel chief absconded with most of his followers' money, and "General" Mosby took command. The Wobblies shot at trains, seized additional supplies and more railway men. After taking over McCormick's train, they steamed southward over the San Diego & Arizona line with 128 "soldiers." But 1,400 Mexican Government troops advancing against them opened fire with machine guns from a hill above the tracks near Frenchman's Ranch. The slaughter was terrific. Federals buried 21 of their own men and a much larger number of rebel dead. The graves, unmarked under the hot desert sun, lie within a few feet of the high iron that now carries freight into and out of Mexico en route between San Diego and California's Imperial Valley.

Mosby and his survivors, fearing capture by the Federals, raced their stolen train back to Tijuana and asked if they could surrender to American forces massed just across the border. This was arranged for. Conductor McCormick had his bullet-ridden train spotted in such a way that his caboose straddled the International Border, with Mosby and his men standing at the Mexican end and Captain Wilcox of the United States Army at the other end. The beaten insurrectionists laid their guns on a table in the waycar at noon of June 22, 1911, and were taken into American custody. Thus a railroad caboose, number and final disposition not recorded, was the scene of an IWW capitulation.

Twenty-two years later the Southern Pacific helped Spreckels to complete the SD&A Railway, bought the stock control, and renamed the line the San Diego & Arizona Eastern.

There's a caboose story behind the world championship bout between Jack Dempsey and Tommy Gibbon at Shelby, Montana, in 1922. Shelby was then an obscure cow-town with dirt streets and about 500 population. Its citizens wanted to stage the fight there because they said "it would put Shelby on the map." The champ's manager, "Doc" Kearns, scoffed at the idea but changed his tune when they offered him a $300,000 guarantee, payable in advance.

Shelby's few business men could raise only $221,000, and the advance sale of 7,202 tickets brought in $70,000 more. Doc agreed to accept $291,000. A wooden arena with 40,000 seats was built but not paid for. Gibbons was to get half of all gate receipts over $300,000. As things turned out, he never got a cent. So many people were broke as a result of the fight that three banks in the area failed. Nobody bought a ticket on the day of the bout. Surging crowds simply pushed down the fence and walked in free. The big event itself was little more than a farce. The Manassa

Mauler barely outpointed the fast-stepping Tommy Gibbons, and spectators hooted in derision.

Anticipating this, Kearns had shrewdly planned a quick getaway, leasing beforehand a 4-4-0 engine and a caboose from the Great Northern which, with the crew's services, cost him $500. Such a movement is known as a caboose hop. The little train waited with steam up. A Federal tax man, also waiting, forced Doc to shell out some $11,000. Then a trunk filled with money in charge of "Nick the Greek," a Dempsey handler, was loaded on the caboose, and the eight-wheeler puffed out of Shelby before the frustrated fight fans knew what was happening.

Another caboose hop, on a blizzard-swept night in 1958, rescued 15 motorists, men and women, who had been stranded in snowdrifts near Sublette, Illinois. Twenty Illinois Central railroaders took part in the operation. The non-paying passengers, weakened by intense cold and hunger, were revived by the genial warmth of a waycar stove and a huge pot of steaming hot coffee. Errands of mercy comparable to this one are fairly common in caboose history.

Bandits have often looted mail and express cars, sometimes robbing passengers also. The only caboose stickup I'm familiar with occurred at night on February 20, 1954, when two thugs wearing plastic hoods and armed with a pistol, a club, and a length of clothesline invaded a crummy. They climbed aboard the rear of a 64-car freight as it was beginning to roll out of the Indiana Harbor Belt yards at Hammond, Indiana. After tying up conductor Ira Budd and his flagman, Len Redding, they took a total of $573 in cash and checks from the railroaders' wallets and then jumped off the slowly-moving train. Budd managed to trip the emergency brake lever with his head, stopping the train in Calumet City. Both crew men freed themselves in time to flag a freight coming up behind them, thus averting a rear-end collision. The robbers were never caught.

No caboose was more closely identified with its conductor than No. 18058 of the Chicago, Rock Island & Pacific. Built in 1904, the

122

Rock Island's famous freight-business-getting caboose, now on display at the National Museum of Transport in St. Louis.—JIM BULLARD

year that a self-reliant young boomer named James P. Bullard went braking on the Rock Island at Eldon, Missouri, it served the road for many years and eventually was pulled out of service, never to run again, the day its conductor, old Jim Bullard, retired.

This caboose was displayed in 1928 at the Missouri State Fair, in 1934 at the Century of Progress Exposition at Chicago, and in 1936 at the International Petroleum Exposition at Tulsa, Oklahoma, and the Texas Centennial celebration. Two years later, a tree was planted in its honor beside the far-away station in Chrysos, Greece, with ceremonies for which the Hellenic State Railways ran special trains and provided speakers. No other caboose has ever attained that kind of distinction.

It all came about because, in 1925, Jim Bullard organized his train crew into a "Get the Business" Committee. Equipping his caboose like an office, he tied down a portable typewriter to a pine board, got paper and other supplies from the Eldon station agent, and set to work. While his train was swinging through the Ozark country along the Missouri and Gascondy rivers, he formulated plans to get freight and passenger business for his road, and wrote letters while it was climbing an 11-mile hill. What correspondence he couldn't finish on his runs Jim took home to Eldon and his daughter Irene, nicknamed "Sunshine," carried on from where he had left off. During layovers of their train at terminals, the crew made personal calls on prospective shippers, using a visiting card which pictured caboose 18058.

Jim Bullard did so well that superintendent George Rourke had him organize other freight crews on his division into business-getting committees. The idea caught on fast. In 1929, despite the onset of the Depression, these committees secured a total of 1,022 cars of freight and 47 cars of passengers—traffic which the CRI&P might never have had otherwise.

The tree planted in Greece honoring the 18058 was a tribute to the charitable work that Jim's crew had done for the Future Farmers clubs of the Near East Foundation in that country. When time finally came for Jim to retire, a great crowd assembled in the St. Louis Union Station, headed by the mayor and Rock Island officials, to greet him and the freshly repainted and redecorated 18058. Today you can see that "little red chariot" at the National Museum of Transport in St. Louis.

Two Illinois Central cabooses rolled to lonely spots in northern Canada in the summer of 1963 so that the University of Illinois scientists could check on an eclipse of the sun. Spotted at Champaign, Illinois, they were fitted with electronic instruments besides the cooking, eating, and sleeping facilities. The first one took off in charge of Wayne Weingarten of the University's Astronomy Department, with three assistants, and was routed over four different railroads to the remote settlement of Moose River in northern Ontario. The second waycar journeyed to Gillam, Manitoba, about halfway up Hudson Bay's western rim, via five railways. Thus, about two weeks before the eclipse, both cabooses were a long way from home.

Those astronomers were interested in what effect the quick shutting off of sunlight would have on the ionosphere and especially its upper regions, about 200 miles above the earth. Normally the cycle from light to darkness takes 24 hours. The eclipse produced the same changes in two and a half hours. University scientists measured the number of electrons in the ionosphere with polarized radio signals reflected from the moon. The use of electronics had an advantage over visual observation in that neither rain nor clouds could interfere with the radio signals they sent up. Afterward, satisfied with their experiments, the men rode back to Champaign in their respective cabooses.

More than $1,000 in U.S. War Bonds and $140 in War Savings Stamps were sold in a single day in 1942 at the dedication of the Alton Railroad's caboose "Victory Car." Painted red, white, and blue, this vehicle bore the words "Buy War Bonds" in letters a foot high. Six other Alton cabooses, similarly painted, also were used to stimulate patriotic sales of bonds and stamps. During World War II, you may remember, the homes of men and women in the armed forces displayed special flags with one star for each person in service. The only caboose to carry such a flag, so far as I know, was the Milwaukee Road's 0673, whose conductor, G. A. Volkman, was proud of the Army record of his furloughed flagman, Gene Kooebel.

The best-known caboose wreck in all history probably would have been forgotten a few months afterward but for a Negro engine-wiper, Wallace Saunders. The caboose was coupled to an Illinois Central freight train in the spring of 1900 and the roundhouse worker was a personal friend of a certain ballast-scorching engineer.

This story has often been told. Passenger train No. 1, *The Cannonball*, with the road's fastest schedule, pulled into Memphis depot late that night of April 29th. The tall, lean, gray-eyed man who took the throttle of engine No. 382 would, if anyone could, make up time as the train sped southward. So *The Cannonball* thundered through the starless night, past station after station; and as the faintly twinkling lights of Durant, Mississippi, fell behind, the six-foot-four hogger called exultantly across the cab to his colored fireman: "The old girl's got her high-heeled slippers on tonight. We ought to make Way on time."

Way is a village six miles north of Canton. The man at the

throttle seemed confident that if he could pass it "on the advertised" he could easily coast into Canton. His McQueen-built ten-wheeler emitted a steady roar from her stack until they reached Vaughan, a dozen miles from Canton. As she swung into a reverse curve, two caboose markers were burning a crimson hole in the night. A freight train pulling into a siding had stopped with its caboose and two boxcars loaded with grain were still on the main line while the crew was chaining up drawheads. ("They didn't put out a flagman," the passenger fireman said later.) Because of the curve, the oncoming engineer couldn't see the caboose lights; but his fireman did, and yelled: "Look out! We're goin' to hit somethin'!"

The hogger shouted back: "Jump, Sim!"

Simeon T. Webb dropped his scoop, leaped wildly, and hit the cinders in the foggy darkness. Engine No. 382 plowed through the caboose and ripped open two boxcars. Aside from a few minor injuries, there was no casualty except the tall engineer. His body was found in the wreckage with an iron bolt driven through his neck and a bale of hay resting on his chest. The dead man was John Luther Jones. A ballad written by Wallace Saunders immortalized his nickname "Casey Jones" in song and story and, indeed, made it part of the English language.

The photographic craftsmanship of Richard Steinheimer produced this most unusual photo deviation of a Colorado & Southern freight train.

Next to the locomotive engineer himself, the most picturesque rail-roader has always been the freight conductor whose business is to boss the train, do the paperwork, assist with switching when necessary, help tie down the hand brakes, lookout for signals and train orders. This Santa Fe Railway conductor happens to be signalling a *Highball.*—DONALD DUKE

SEVEN

Romance, Childbirth, and Murder

IN ADDITION to their railroad uses, cabooses have been the
scene of elopements, marriages, childbirth, suicide, and even
murder. Let's start with an episode in which I was personal-
ly involved on the old single-tracked Oklahoma-Southwestern,
long since abandoned.

Mike Clancy, short but powerfully built, was the O-SW section
foreman at Wren, in the wheat belt. Wren consisted of a tiny
wooden depot with a telegraph office, a sun-blistered wooden water
tank bound with iron rings, a few frame dwellings for section
hands, a grain elevator, and that was about all. Mike's only
daughter, Nora, redheaded and blue-eyed like himself, fell in love
with Tony Guilia, a young fireman. Not wanting Tony for a
son-in-law, the old man forebade him to see Nora or communicate
with her in any way. But somehow the fireman managed to visit
her on the sly. That was the situation when I hired out to the
O-SW as a conductor for the wheat rush.

Just before we pulled out of Rawson terminal one day, Tony
came into my caboose. "I'm asking a favor of you, Mr. Knapke,"
he said hesitantly, "because you're a boomer and won't be here

Mississippian Railway is a rather long name to stencil on the side of this classic wood caboose. So an abbreviation was in order, prompting an untoward nickname of *Misery* and the far kinder *Miss Ry.*—JOHN KRAUSE

long anyway, and I wouldn't want any regular conductor to get into trouble. I know you don't give a damn."

"Maybe not," I parried, "but what's the favor?"

Tony and Nora planned to elope and wanted to ride my caboose. "If we take a passenger train at Wren," he explained, "everybody would know about it and the old man would wire ahead to stop us, 'cause Nora isn't 18 yet."

I said gravely: "Tony, how do I know you'll marry the girl?"

He beamed as he showed me a marriage license, properly signed. "All right," I said, and we made plans. That day my orders called for picking up two cars of wheat at Wren. I went to the office for the waybills while my brakeman was coupling on the cars and while the engine, an American type, was taking water. Returning to the caboose, I found the loving couple there with a big suitcase, waiting for us, but Nora was worried.

"I just saw a section man ride off on a pony," she said. "I know he's going to tell Dad," her voice faltered, "and Dad will make me get off the train and go home."

"But suppose he doesn't find you here?"

Her blue eyes widened. "What do you mean, Mr. Knapke? How could we hide on the train?"

There was only one place to hide. Each loaded boxcar was sealed with a lead button, through which passed a hairpin-shaped wire and on which a sealing-iron had imprinted a number. This showed whether or not the car was opened en route. But every boomer I have known had a bag of tricks, and I was a boomer. Taking a saw-blade knife from my grip, I sawed off the seal from the rear door of the car just ahead of the caboose, opened the door wide enough to let the elopers crawl in on top of the wheat, and bade them keep quiet. Then I replaced the lead button, squeezing the sawed ends of wire together so that the seal, unless closely inspected, would not reveal tampering.

Nora's hunch was right. Three miles from Wren the section boss flagged us and boarded the caboose, bellowing, "Where's my daughter?" I played dumb, of course.

Mike peered into our closets and lockers. "She ain't here," he raved, "but sure as hell she's somewhere on this train."

"She's not in the engine cab, either," I said, "and every car is loaded with wheat and locked and sealed."

He stormed up to the head end, didn't find the girl, and returned to the crummy, glaring angrily at the seals as he went by.

I looked at my watch. "Number 7's due here in 15 minutes," I warned. "If you keep us much longer I'll stick that passenger train and you'll have to answer for it."

Just then our hogger blew three short whistle blasts and a long one, the signal for a flagman to walk *ahead*, on the single-tracked line, to protect the train.

"All right then, go on!" the old man growled. "But I still know you've got Nora hid somewhere."

I gave the peaked end a highball and we got rolling again. As we passed the next telegraph office, the operator handed me this message: "Clancy told Wren to wire ahead to have bull search your train for unauthorized passengers."

After reading it, I put my face close to the end door of the car ahead and asked, "Can you kids hear me?" and then I told them what had happened. Sure enough, after we had gone down the line a few more stations, a special agent named Mark Owens climbed into the crummy. But Mark was a good scout. I explained about the romance and he didn't search very hard.

"Mike must be off his rocker," he chuckled as he left us, adding in a low voice, "Give the love birds my best wishes."

When we pulled up at Etoah, end of the line, a surrey with a team of bay horses was waiting for the excited young couple. Tony lugged the heavy suitcase down the caboose steps. Nora said, with misty eyes: "Thank you, Mr. Knapke. We'll never forget your kindness." And she threw her slender arms around me and kissed me. I never saw either of them again.

A less conventional romance centered around an unconventional caboose on the Georgia Northern shortly after that pioneer logging road had become a common carrier. Here is the story as I got it from conductor Edwards:

The waycar was a doghouse type, just a square boxlike hut built on one end of a short flatcar, the other end being piled with chains, knuckles, coupling pins, and other hardware plus, at times, LCL freight to be dropped off at way stations. You had to climb over a lot of junk to get into or out of it. Not only that, but this caboose also accommodated passengers now and then, if "accommodated" is the right word.

The crew included Edwards; his flagman, Clem Smith, fresh from the farm, handsome and amiable, and a Negro brakeman named Calvin. At that time a woodburning 4-4-0 pulled the train. The engineer was Charlie Pope, an ordained minister who had never filled a pulpit. He and his fireman, Ernie Piland, liked to "wood up" at Sumlers, a village which had been furnishing cordwood to the Georgia Northern for about 20 years, before it began using coal. The entire crew was supposed to help load the wood, except Clem Smith, who was a privileged character because he often supplied "the boys" with watermelons and canteloupes.

Edwards never questioned what his flagman did so long as he kept other woodburners from plowing into their rear. One day, however, the conductor wasn't feeling so well and asked Clem to help with the wooding. While the rest of the crew were filling the tender with short logs, Edwards sat down on a pile of old cross-ties under a pine tree, watching two chipmunks at play. To his surprise, a shapely young female figure emerged suddenly from a clump of gallberry bushes, looking timid and about to cry. He recognized her as Clem's girl and asked: "What's the matter, Carrie?"

The girl hung her head. After Edwards had repeated the question, she blurted out: "I want you to make Clem marry me, Mr. Edwards, afore Pa gets wind of what we did and goes after him with a shotgun."

The skipper thought a moment. They went into details and then he said: "You meet us here tomorrow afternoon at this time, Carrie, and I'll see what can be done."

He knew that Clem Smith had got into a scrap at Moultrie, the county seat, and the police chief had threatened to jail the young fireman next time he showed up in that town; so even if Clem wanted to, he couldn't get a marriage license there. The conductor went into a huddle with the engine crew. Ernie Piland had a friend in the courthouse and promised to get the license. Charlie Pope was a bit dubious about his ministerial standing but agreed to perform the wedding ceremony if Clem could be persuaded.

The California redwood forest at Sequoia returns to deep eternal silence after a Northwestern Pacific wood crummy clatters by.—DICK STEINHEIMER

"He will," Edwards said firmly.

The following afternoon Carrie, clad in her white Sunday-go-to-meetin' dress and looking real pretty, climbed over the pile of hardware into the caboose, and the flagman's jaw dropped with astonishment.

"What are you doin' here, Carrie?" he asked.

The girl explained briefly. "You and me is gettin' married today and here's our license," showing him the document.

Thereupon the conductor blocked the front and back doors to discourage any possible idea of running away that might enter the head of the prospective groom and father-to-be. After shooting his mouth off and trying to push Edwards aside, Clem caught the appealing look in Carrie's eyes and quickly simmered down.

"I'll do it, Carrie," he said. "I'll wed you. Honest to God I will, but what about a ring?"

The other men looked blankly at one another. Then Ernie, fumbling in his overalls pocket, fished out a little brass ring, a packing ring for a lubricator feed glass, and asked, "Will this do?"

It would—and did. Charlie Pope cleared his throat. "Clem Smith, when you take this solemn legal oath of wedlock, all of us aim to see that you keep it. Is that clear?"

Clem smiled at the girl. "Yes," he said, "and I'll be as good to her as my ornery disposition'll let me—and I mean it."

Charlie Pope, hogger and "sky pilot," tied the knot in a hurry, because his train was blocking the main line, with no flag out.

The sawmill settlement of Fort Seward, California, was water-logged late one January afternoon when a Northwestern Pacific freight train of 54 cars pulled out in charge of conductor Clarence W. Renwick. Rain had been falling steadily for days. Highways were impassible and the roadbed was so soft that trains had to creep over most of the division. Renwick had his clearances and waybills. He stood on the depot platform and as the two 4600 class diesels on his train rumbled slowly by he handed the engineer a copy of the clearances, saying: "Take it easy, so I can catch the crummy."

Car after car rolled by at a leisurely gait, the conductor survey-ing each one by his lantern light. Almost the entire train had passed when the station agent, W. R. Kelly, dashed out of his office, yelling: "Hey, Renwick, my wife's about to have a baby!"

"That so?" the skipper said calmly. "Congratulations, and what am I supposed to do about it?"

"Take her to the hospital, Clarence. I can't get there by auto—wagon road's washed out."

Renwick's lantern swung a quick stop sign, but by that time the two 4600's were around a curve and out of sight. He shouted to his rear brakeman in the caboose: "Pull the air, Martin! Pull the air!"

The wheels screeched and stood still. Kelly helped his pregnant wife into the waycar, made her comfortable on a locker, and sat down beside her. Meanwhile, Martin was running up to the head end to explain what had happened. Then he came back to the caboose and seated himself in the cupola. While Renwick was writing his reports the lady let out a scream. Kelly paced the floor helplessly. The conductor went into action. He had already put two buckets of water on the stove, just in case. Now he jerked the mattress from his bunk onto the floor.

"Oh, Martin," he called up, "come down and give me a hand!"

The brakeman took a fast disconcerting glance. "Not me, mister! I think we've got a hotbox about 50 cars ahead. I gotta go see about it." And away he went over the tops, muttering to himself.

Renwick had no medical or surgical equipment to work with, only a pair of wick-trimming scissors, which he sterilized in scalding water, and a spool of khaki thread, but he did the best he could. Later, when the train stopped at Scotia and the road's general manager, George L. Morrison, came rushing into the caboose, the tired conductor nervously handed him a baby boy to take out to a waiting ambulance. Mrs. Kelly was carried out on a stretcher, "doing nicely, thank you."

I often think of a fast caboose run to a hospital one sultry afternoon out of Yuma, Arizona, enroute to Indio, California, with me as a Southern Pacific conductor and the weather hotter'n the hinges of hell—mercury 115 to 120 with high humidity, which was mighty hard to take. After crossing the swift Colorado River that glittered like fire in the bright sun, we were flagged at the foot of Aras Hill and informed that the heat had knocked out Jimmie

The view from the cupola is like a private Vista Dome car. The scene above is from the deck of a Canadian National van which is about to enter a solid rock bore between Moncton and Edmundston. — PHIL HASTINGS (*Below*) The grandeur of Colorado's Rocky Mountains from a Colorado & Southern freight near Climax.—HENRY R. GRIFFITHS

Gratto, our superintendent of bridges and building. So we took him aboard.

My caboose, No. 339, had side as well as end doors. I laid the mattress from my bunk on the floor between the two side doors, which I kept open to let in whatever tiny wisps of breeze might be drifting over the sun-baked desert. Some empty refrigerator cars had a little icewater left in their bunkers. I told the parlor man to wet a sheet in icewater. We draped it over the patient, wrapped an icy-wet towel around his head like a turban, and lit out for Ogilby, the next telegraph office. There I notified the dispatcher that I wanted a clear track to Indio and the hospital; and he put three eastward trains, a passenger and two freights, "in the hole" for us.

Instead of taking my entire train, I left most of it at Ogilby, keeping only the engine, a low-wheeled Mikado freight hog, and ten steel-wheeled oil tanks for braking purposes. Well, sir, we averaged 69 miles per hour from Ogilby to Indio, which was the talk of the division for a long time afterward. Our engineer had his throttle wide open all the way, with no stops for meets, and ended his speedy run with the caboose spotted right in front of the hospital. Jimmie Gratto was a small man with a spare build, as I am, and I carried him in my arms into the hospital, where a nurse took charge of him. A few days later Jimmie was up and around. He often said I had saved his life with a combination of ice and high speed.

Sometimes a caboose taxi run is pleasant. For example, when actress Anita Stewart set out on a journey to keep an engagement at a summer theater, a ticket agent said she could change trains at Iowa Falls, Iowa; but when she arrived there she learned with dismay that regular passenger trains out of the town had been discontinued some time before, and she completed her trip to Estherville, Iowa, in a Rock Island caboose. Later she enthused, "Those wonderful Rock Island men even treated me to dinner while I was waiting for someone to come and pick me up."

Back in 1912, on one of the very rare occasions other than train wrecks when death rode the waycar, a drunken sheepherder was killed in a caboose brawl on the old Duluth, Memphis & Atlantic

138

(now part of the Missouri Pacific). Maybe some oldtimer can supply the missing details. Another caboose fight that led to a killing occurred at Vaughn, New Mexico. The conductor, Sam Cotton, was operating waycar 797 on the second district of the Southern Pacific's Pecos Division between Vaughn and Belen, with brakeman Moore and Babier. The last-named was a giant of six-feet two, a former engineer who had transferred to train service. According to I. L. Sears, who was braking on the division at that time, this is what happened:

Both Moore and Babier had a reputation for heavy drinking. One night, following a booze party, they went to bed in the 797, apparently got into a drunken argument, and Moore was beaten into unconsciousness. Not long afterward, evidently while Babier was asleep in his bunk, he was shot dead with four bullets from a Smith & Wesson .38. The sheriff arrested Moore, charged him with the crime, and held him in jail at Fort Sumner for several days.

"I saw him being transferred from Fort Sumner to the Santa Rosa lockup," said Sears. "Poor fellow, he still showed the effects of the terrific beating he'd received. You'd think he had been run through a meat-grinder. The railroaders on our division had a lot of sympathy for Moore. Somehow he escaped from jail, maybe with the help of one or two of them, and none of us have heard of him since."

Many years ago Frank McConnell, conductor on another SP division, the Shasta, fell in love with his caboose No. 117, and began fixing it up to suit his own ideas, as was customary in those days. His "honeymoon" with the 117 was long and happy. But the inexorable passage of years changes all things and the company decided to scrap his outmoded old hack. Frank was desperate. He pleaded and argued with the brass collars, so they finally relented and let it remain in operation until he was ready for a pension.

The skipper sighed with relief and continued to work and relax in the old familiar vehicle. At length, just after his retirement, the 117 was taken out of service and set on the rip track to be junked. The aging man was frantic. He visited it daily until the actual dismantling started. Then, as the wreckers were tearing his beloved caboose to pieces, Frank McConnell entered the 117 for the

The pattern of railroading hadn't changed for half a century when this pastoral scene was photographed along Rock Island's faltering Postville Branch. The agent watches his daily duties leave town as the conductor steps aboard his hack.—PHIL HASTINGS

last time, with a hidden revolver. Pretty soon the workmen heard a shot. Rushing into the partly-demolished car, they found the grayheaded conductor in a pool of blood, dying. Frank just couldn't take it, so he went out with the 117.

Romance, childbirth, taxi service, and death by violence—all are part of the caboose story. There is also a murder mystery. One of the worst blizzards in years was keeping the Missouri Pacific's rotary plows busy that cold night of December 9, 1932, when Chris Lavoo's freight train crawled into Horace, Kansas, at 11:50. Heavy drifts had retarded it to such an extent that the crew's working time under the 16-hour law had nearly expired. So the dispatcher tied them up for a much-needed eight hours of rest. Chris elected to spend the night in his waycar. His two brakemen, well bundled up, bade him goodnight and plodded wearily uptown to get beds in a rooming-house.

Next morning at 7:30 a switchman named Glen Neil, peeping through the glass of the caboose door, saw the dead body of conductor Lavoo, clad in pajamas, crumpled in a corner. The door was locked, having a latch that could be opened only from the inside without a key but which would lock automatically when it closed. A revolver lay on the floor; ballistics tests later proved it was the murder weapon. There was unmistakable evidence of a struggle but no clue of the killer's identity or motive.

Company records show that Christopher Lavoo had been in Missouri Pacific train service for 18 years and he was generally regarded as a kindly man, with no enemies, who had been living happily in Pueblo, Colorado, with his wife, his son, and two daughters. A third daughter was married. Except for the murderer, whoever he or she may have been, Chris's two brakemen were almost certainly the last persons to have seen him alive. Till this day the crime has never been solved.

Rail and river traffic was tied up for a day in August 1941, when this Pere Marquette train with caboose A-386 backed into an open drawbridge at Grand Haven, Michigan.

EIGHT

Guardian Angels

TRAINMEN who railroaded from the rear end in bygone days had a particular dread of runaways and collisions. Many an oldtimer believed he escaped disaster or came out of a caboose wreck unscathed because "my guardian angel was riding the crummy." I am reminded of W. J. Cotter's experience when he was braking on the Delaware & Hudson one summer night in 1917.

"We were doubleheading north from Oneonta, New York," he told me, "with an 87-car train, mostly boxcars loaded with merchandise. Due to the wartime scarcity of help, an extra engineer was running the head engine and handling the air. East Worcester to Cobleskill was ten miles of steep descending grade. Trains made a full stop before going down. That night, as usual, we stopped at the summit. While the runner on the first engine was pumping up his train-line again, I stepped off the caboose and walked along the southbound track halfway to the head end so as to inspect the brake rigging and set up retainers before we headed downhill.

"Well, at West Richmondville, about a mile down the grade, the hogger set the brakes as usual. At first we slowed down but after a few hundred yards we picked up speed. At this point the block signal indicated caution. As I learned later, the hogger applied his air again but with no effect. Looking at my watch, I figured that southbound No. 12 from Albany was already due at Richmondville, which was dead ahead, and our hogger would have to be an artist to make a quick stop if he should see her there.

"The next block also showed caution. Somewhat alarmed at not hearing a call for brakes, I walked over the tops of the few cars that separated me from the caboose and I rapped on the roof to get the conductor's attention. He yelled up at me: 'Set up those brakes damn quick! The gauge here shows only ten pounds of air!' and with that he climbed through the cupola onto the roof of the last boxcar. I knew he had a brake club, so I made my way up ahead to where I could be of more use.

"Hearing an engine, I glanced around and saw we were just passing between Richmondville depot and train 12, standing on the southbound track. Even then, for some reason unknown to me, our engineer hadn't signaled for brakes. I started winding up brakes about 20 cars ahead of the caboose, working toward the engine. The block still showed caution. Evidently another train dropping downhill in front of us was running as fast as our train. About three miles below Richmondville depot the right-of-way sags for some distance and when we hit the uphill side we dragged to a nice stop.

"Without a warning whistle from the hogger, we had been drifting down the grade just as if we had no engine. At Cherry Valley, half a mile further on, I began walking forward over the train in hopes of solving the mystery. When we pulled down to the tower, two red lights in the darkness showed a caboose there. By that time the engineer and conductor had settled their differences. I was instructed to switch our engines around, putting the second locomotive in front, as the extra hogger on the first one was incapable of running the hills. While we were waiting for a clear track I hiked on ahead to chin with the flagman of the train holding us up."

Then, Cotter told me, he learned what might have happened and his heart skipped a beat. The flagman had been riding the caboose top because of a hotbox, and he said: "Damn fool engineer, running wild! He never looked back, even once. I wish they'd make hoggers ride backward down these hills so they could see the hind end."

Cotter concluded: "I shudder to think of the pile-up that would have resulted if that 'damn fool engineer' had stopped at Richmondville, with us coming up right behind and unable to stop and with train 12 standing on the other track. My guardian angel must have been riding the crummy that night."

And was there a guardian angel on duty aboard a certain Union Pacific freight train in Wyoming more than 40 years later? K. N. Knowlson, the head brakeman, thought there was. He recalled that they were descending a slight grade into Bridger station, with the slack bunching toward the engine as usual, and this forced the caboose to run into the car ahead, which lifted an under-slung pin and separated the caboose from the train. When the air-brake went into emergency, Knowlson looked back from the engine cab and was surprised to see the waycar standing still by itself about a half-mile back of the train.

Conductor G.E. Mourey and his flagman, E. Barnes, slowed the hack by applying the hand-brake. Then Barnes got off and bled the air-brakes off so that the caboose moved down to the train and coupled into the car from which it had been separated. After that, with air restored, the train resumed its trip with no further incident.

Remember the earthquake, back in the fifties, which disrupted Southern Pacific-Santa Fe joint operations over the Tehachapi Mountains in California? One SP freight train broke in two and the three diesel-electric locomotives used as helpers on the rear stopped in a tunnel. The diesel fumes were so suffocating that the engine crews walked ahead to the tunnel mouth to breathe fresh air. Of course, the three helpers had the slack shoved up tight, and the brakes going into emergency held them in that position. With the recoupling and the air cut in, the brakes released and the rear end rolled back. The weight of the three diesels was too much for the coupling to hold. The knuckle broke and away they went, shoving the caboose before them. As they passed, the flagman tried to climb aboard, but the speed was too great.

Meanwhile, a following Santa Fe freight had stopped at an automatic block signal. Its fireman, looking ahead, saw the diesels and a caboose approaching on the same track at what he judged to be 50 miles per hour, and yelled: "Unload! They're onto us!" He jumped, followed by the head brakeman. The engineer slammed the train brakes into emergency and then hit the ground running. Caught in the middle, the waycar collapsed into a pile of splintered wood and twisted steel.

Casualties ran high in the days before air-brakes and automatic couplers, but nearly all of the caboose wrecks and runaways since then have stopped short of disaster. One case comes to mind, though, when the lack of modern safety devices was not involved and the presence of a guardian angel would have been very helpful.

During World War I the Northern Pacific was running eastbound dead freight out of Pasco, Washington, on the Spokane, Portland & Seattle line, which is pretty much of a water-level route. One day a Pasco supply man made the fatal mistake of putting a two-gallon can of distillate, instead of signal oil, in a caboose. Distillate is similar to gasoline and is fuel for the speeders used by section men. It does not belong in a caboose. A few miles out of Farrington, dusk overtook the drag that was carrying this two-gallon can. When, on a high bridge, the unsuspecting flagman tried to fill the marker lights and lanterns, the distillate exploded with a blinding flash. Leaping out the rear door in terror, he flagged a local freight and rode home to Pasco. Hours passed before the rest of the crew learned where he was.

Meanwhile, the blast had set the caboose afire. The conductor and the swing man, both painfully burned, tore off their blazing clothes. Stark naked except for shoes and socks, they sought refuge on the boxcar roofs. After much delay, the engine crew cut off the waycar and last three cars, to which the flames had spread. Then they assisted the conductor and swing man into the engine cab, and their hand-fired Mikado made a fast run to the nearest doctor, there being in that area practically no automobiles and no good roads. After picking up a physician, they placed him and the two patients in a boxcar and cut loose for Spokane. They made it in record time, but the two victims died in a hospital the next day. Charles E. Cunningham, now a retired NP engineer, who told me the story, didn't say a word about guardian angels.

Just about the worst messed-up hack I ever saw was one I rode in on the Espee many years ago. Our caboose and two cars, released from work-train service, were returning to the terminal at about 18 miles per hour over a branch line which had no carded trains, when we came to a washout. The engineer, Sol Woods, said afterward that he'd felt the engine lurch and drop. By jerking open the throttle, he got her over the flooded section, but the water-car fell into a hole about ten feet deep and rammed into a solid bank of earth, causing a stop somewhat sooner than instantaneous.

Everything in the caboose moved forward. The stove, fortunately cold, was uprooted from the floor while the desk was torn off the wall. Cupboards and lockers were broken, water barrels and washstand piled up grotesquely, and the bunks were demolished. In fact, everything, not omitting the train crew, went to the front end of the caboose with such speed that we didn't know what had happened. The tongue-and-groove siding was at a 60-degree angle, with the rear truck against the possum belly but, aside from a few bruises, nobody was hurt. Strangely, the markers remained lighted.

There have been many freak train wrecks, but the one Charlie Timlin told me about comes near the top of the list. Charlie is an old retired boomer conductor. Back in May 1910, while braking behind on the Chicago, Peoria & St. Louis line, he tried to light a gasoline stove in the caboose somewhere between Kilbourne and Petersburg, Illinois. The stove gave a terrifying *whoosh!* and the whole inside of the crummy looked like an erupting volcano.

Charlie didn't linger. After diving through a caboose window, he gave the head end a series of frantic stop signals, but apparently nobody saw them and there was no continuous air-line on the train, so he couldn't pull the air. Just as the caboose topped a hill it burned in two. Debris piling in front of the rear truck halted that part of the crummy; but the front half stayed with the train up to the point where they stopped for water, a short distance from the foot of the hill.

The guardian angel, if any, saved Charlie, the other brakeman, and the conductor. All three stood in a daze, gaping at what was left of their parlor. Someone yelled. The rear truck, bounding down the grade like a bat outa hell, smashed into the head part of the caboose. The debris that had halted the truck at the summit

Time was running out for the long supremacy of steam when Central Vermont's north and southbound milk trains Nos. 211 and 210 passed each other at Waterbury, Vermont, back in 1950.—PHIL HASTINGS

had burned away, releasing the truck and letting it roll. I am quite sure there is no other case on record of a waycar colliding with itself!

Another oddity was the wreck that demolished four hacks in one fell swoop on a warm, sunny, May day in 1964. Operations were proceeding normally in the Jersey Central's sprawling yard at Allentown, Pennsylvania. At about 11 a.m. the eastbound hump slipped a caboose into a storage track, coupling it into three other waycars already on the siding. Then the crew went for a string of freight cars to classify on the hump. Returning with this string, the diesel yard goat ran into the storage track, through a switch carelessly left open, with the result I have mentioned.

Luckily, all four crummies were empty. A wooden one ended up at the bottom of the heap with two others perched on its flattened car-body. Hot coals in the stove set fire to the wreckage, and the local fire department was called. Adding to Jersey Central's embarrassment was the fact that three of the wrecked cabooses belonged to the Reading Railroad, which also used the Allentown yard.

Fred Knight, a Canadian Pacific conductor, was running over the Colonsay subdivision in Saskatchewan one dark night when his air-line became disconnected and the train broke in two with the uncoupling of the caboose (which our Canadian friends call a van). Well, the crew recoupled the train and proceeded to Colonsay. There they discovered they were short one car. Greatly puzzled, they went back over the line the following morning, keeping a sharp lookout for the missing vehicle, and at length they found it —out in a field near the village of Holdfast, where the train had broken in two the night before. But how it had gotten away in the darkness is still a mystery.

The freakiest wreck I ever heard of occurred on the Blackwell, Enid & South Western (now Frisco Lines) about two miles out of Beaumont, Texas. A freight train collided with a car of black powder in the summer of 1903. Although the caboose was 30 car-lengths away, its inside was so scorched by the explosion as to require repainting. But here's the peculiar feature: according to an Interstate Commerce Commission report, the caboose curtains were of a heavy and thickly-striped material somewhat like bed

One of the pleasant sides of caboose life is to sit in the "doghouse" (cupola) watch the world roll by. This brakeman on California's Sunset Railway (joint S; Fe-Southern Pacific) checks his consist for a possible hotbox.—STAN KISTLER

ticking, and the blast ripped every curtain along each and every stripe, from top to bottom, as cleanly as if cut with scissors!

One day on the Cotton Belt, when I was the parlor brakeman, the guardian angel must have been dozing. As we neared Louisville Junction, where the Shreveport branch angles off the main line, I was seated in the cupola enjoying the scenery as the conductor worked on his reports. Something odd happened. The engine continued on toward Texarkana, Texas, but the tender decided to go to Shreveport, Louisiana. Naturally, we stopped with abruptness.

My legs were extended cozily on the "lazy board" when the sudden impact knocked me out for a moment. When I came to, I heard strong language from the skipper. The jar had upturned his chair and skidded his head and shoulders under the stove—a type with legs instead of the common solid base. Somehow his own legs had been thrust through the chair rungs in such a manner as to prevent his getting leverage to work his way out from beneath the stove. One of his ears was torn and bleeding.

Although I felt sorry for his injury, the sight of him wedged in that crazy position struck me as comical, but I choked back a laugh. If I had let out one little snicker the old man would have made a whistling post out of me. I grabbed his ankles and pulled him into the clear and while I was doing so he cursed the stove fluently.

"You're lucky it has an open base," I said. "If it hadn't, you'd probably have a broken neck."

Another incident that tickled my funny-bone occurred at Ordway, California, on the western slope of San Gorgonio Pass where SP crossed the San Bernardino Mountains. That afternoon I was skippering a freight that took siding for passenger train No. 4. We waited there long enough for all the retainers to leak off, and when we started again the train hit a fast clip. I stood on the caboose rear platform with my back against the wall. Frank Lillis, my rear brakeman, was down on the steps, ready to get off and close the switch. The engineer made an air reduction to slow the train.

What ensued is described technically as "an undesired triple action"; trainmen refer to it as "a damn dynamiter." The hind end of that crummy bounced several feet upward, tossing Frank off the steps. He lit on his feet, thanks maybe to his guardian angel, but how he stayed on them I'll never know. He spun around, pirouetting first on one foot and then the other, bowed, and whirled like a dancing dervish until he was brought up against the right-of-way fence.

As he clung to the fence, waiting for his head to clear, a pigtailed little girl with big blue eyes, standing in the doorway of a cottage nearby, ran over to Frank and asked: "Mister, will you please do that again so mamma can see it?" For a moment the brakeman glared at the child; then he laughed until tears rolled down his cheeks. For some time afterwards we kidded him with, "Do that again so mamma can see it."

Not very far from that spot, in the windy darkness of a summer night in 1910, a Southern Pacific freight with three engines belching great clouds of smoke stormed up the western slope of the pass in charge of conductor Carothers. The crew held an order that required them to wait, until a specified time, at Hinda for an opposing train. Coming into Hinda, the engineer eased off on his throttle, slowed to a crawl, and stopped for ten minutes. Shortly before that time expired, he whistled in the flag, figuring it would take about three minutes for the flagman, Ed Kammerling, to return. Pretty soon the swift up-and-down motion of a light at the rear told him that Ed was in and to "take 'em away."

The helper engines' whistles said that they, too, were ready and so the road hogger opened his throttle. At that moment a grim sound of rending timbers and iron indicated that the strain had torn out the rear drawbar of the fifth car. Carothers had just walked up to the head end, intending to ride the engine to Beaumont at the top of the grade, so he was present to give instructions. He decided to set out the bad-order car, just into clear, on the passing siding and then to have the train pull up over the switch and pick up the car behind the caboose.

As the drawbar on the forward end of the crippled car was intact, that was the right decision. Accordingly, the BO was placed on the siding; the swing brakeman climbed on top and set the hand-brake. Just as the locomotive and four cars returned to the rest of the train, the BO began rolling down the grade. The conductor and head brakeman had their backs to it, so the engineer was the first to notice what was happening. He yelled and pointed at the moving car.

With a quick sprint, Carothers and the brakeman caught the runaway, climbed aboard, and doubled on the hand-brake but to no avail. Outside, a gale was whistling and howling. Faster and faster the maverick rolled. At length, seeing that the brake had no effect, the two men jumped off. But before Carothers left, he hastily bent the wire handle of his lantern into a hook and hung it on the brake-wheel in the hope that he might give at least a brief warning to a following train before the almost inevitable collision.

Meanwhile the parlor man, Ed Kammerling, was standing near the rear steps of his caboose, No. 253, on the main line. His ears told him what was going on at the head end and his eyes were fixed on the sky behind, watching for a headlight glare reflected against the clouds that would denote a following train. Looking backward, he failed to see the dark, quietly-rolling mass of the runaway car until it was right at him. Then he spied the gleam of Carothers' lamp on top.

By that time the maverick was doing 40 or 50 miles an hour. As it swerved from the siding to the main stem, the partly-applied hand-brake forced the brake-shoes to grip the wheels a bit tighter, ejecting a pinwheel of sparks. Ed thought some crew member was on the runaway and unable to get off, due to the high speed. Maybe he could get the man off, whoever he might be, before it was too late. His caboose was a heavy, old-fashioned type with free-moving passenger trucks. He turned the quick-bleed valve on its air-brake; then he ran to the front and jerked the cutoff. The well-oiled lock worked instantly; the caboose began to roll.

Ed sprang aboard, opened doors and windows to lessen air resistance, grabbed a brake club, and hurried out to the front platform. Then he untied and took with him a length of bell-cord that the crew had been using as a clothes-line. On the platform, he lashed himself to the hand-rail, knowing that enormous wind pressure would develop at high speed. He set the lantern on the floor between his feet and stared ahead. The race was on!

Faster and faster rail-joints clicked under wheels racing through the dark night. The wind moaned. A crash like hollow thunder denoted the rush over a steel bridge. At length, rounding a curve,

Ed caught sight of the gallivanting boxcar as it fled around another curve. Gradually he gained on it. The night operator, an open telegraph office midway up the western slope, was playing checkers by wire with a distant fellow night-hawk. Puzzled by what he heard, for no train was due, he reached for the dispatcher's key to inquire. But before he could make the first click, the ground vibrated, windows rattled, and two dark objects several yards apart shot by his office; so he wired the dispatcher:

"Clear main line two runaway cars speed 125 mph."

Long before Ed got to El Casco, his lantern had jiggled to the edge of the platform and fallen off and the gale had extinguished the marker lights, leaving him in total darkness. By the time he reached the west end of the siding, the way car lacked but a few feet of coupling into the car ahead. Soon the couplers closed and locked.

Ed swung onto the caboose brake with all his might. A little past Ordway he had things under control. The two cars drifted to the next siding, Brookside, and stopped gently near a telephone booth. Ed Kammerling got off and went to the phone to ask about train 244 that he knew was coming toward him on the single-track main, somewhere back in the darkness.

Meanwhile, preparations were being made to stop all traffic over railroad street crossings and the Pacific Electric Railway tracks, and the tower operator of the Santa Fe's interlocking plant cleared a route for the runaways. The yardmaster realized that the steep grade west of Colton would slow them materially and he had an engine standing on a spur in readiness to chase them. These preparations completed, the railroaders waited tensely. At length a telephone rang. From the receiver came a calm voice:

"This is brakeman Kammerling with a caboose and a runaway car on the main line at Brookside. Where'n hell is 244?"

Ed attributed the good luck to his guardian angel. And now for a story about another runaway. The Southern Pacific's little yard at Santa Monica, California, stood near the edge of a slope. You didn't cut cars there without someone to ride 'em—that is, not more than once. A freight engine went into the Santa Monica terminal one night with only the waycar—a "caboose hop," we call it. Since the brakeman lived but two city blocks from the tracks, conductor O. I. Lockwood dropped him off opposite his home, saving him a long walk from the yard.

The other brakeman, Charlie Freeman, lined the yard switches for the engine to push the caboose onto a spur track and hollered to the skipper, "All yours, Lock," and cut the waycar loose. Quickly it gained speed as it shot down the spur. When Lockwood was signing his last report, ready to put the caboose away, he heard a screeching and the rending of timbers and sank back in his chair. Then, rushing out to the rear platform, he found that the caboose had gone through the sandbox butting post. All four sets of its steps had been shorn off and it was standing in disgrace with its front wheels resting against the curb on the far side of Santa Fe Boulevard—and Lockwood still aboard!

A Pacific Electric owl car had stopped a few feet away, its headlight glare shining reproachfully at the crummy that blocked its passage. Well, the wayward caboose was finally hauled back onto the rails, and Los Angeles shopmen replaced its missing steps while the section gang rebuilt the butting post. No official report was made of the mishap. As I said, it isn't safe to cut a car off unless there's a man at the brakewheel, but maybe if your guardian angel is hovering around there won't be a tragedy.

Bloodless accidents are commonplace. More than one crummy has fallen into a river, lake, or bay and the occupants jumped in time or swam ashore safely. Up in Maine long ago the Portland & Rumford Falls built a waycar with a high cupola in their own shops, numbered it 6, and assigned it to Rumford-Lewiston local freight. On its very first run the cupola was ripped off by a low bridge in Lewiston, but nobody was hurt. The home-made hack, given a new lower cupola, remained in service until the Maine Central took over the P&RF in 1907 and scrapped it.

Even a tornado doesn't necessarily spill blood. One very hot summer day in 1955 a Northern Pacific local freight was jogging along toward Mandan, North Dakota, making occasional setouts and pickups. Seated in the doghouse, brakeman Charlie Lewis was mopping his brow while the conductor, Sam Arliss, worked listlessly at his desk. A peculiar humming assailed their ears. Still miles behind them but rapidly approaching was a twisting, writhing column of dust that reached high in the air. Charlie leaped from the sun parlor and stood beside his skipper at the rear door, watching tensely.

The hum became a roar, then a howl as the spiral of dirty wind overtook the train. Inside, the caboose became black as night. A grinding jar gave the two men the impression that their car had left the rails and was bumping along the ties. Then the vehicle seemed to be spinning like a top. It hurled the frightened men onto the lockers, which they clutched grimly. The caboose had been lifted into the air! At length, with a mild thump the tornado veered away from the railroad to spread destruction elsewhere. Its freakish play with the waycar had been merely an interlude.

The little red chariot was intact, not even a window broken or cracked, but when the railroaders finally opened the door and looked out it was resting on farmland a good 500 feet from the track! What really astonished Sam Arliss, though, was the fact that his papers remained on the desk as they had been before the disturbance! Two cars had been overturned but the rest of the train was undamaged, and there were no casualties in the crew. No doubt about it, Sam and Charlie will always remember their ride in a flying caboose.

Another big wind is recalled by E. J. Mathiesen. "Many years ago," he told me, "I was firing a diamond-stack ten-wheeler for engineer Tipton on the Missouri Pacific in western Kansas. We were bucking a stiff head-wind about two miles out of Tribune, our division point. I noticed a car on the main stem that seemed to be getting larger all the time, although no engine was visible, and I yelled to Tipton, 'Looks like that car is coming right at us!' He stopped the train. We were about to unload when we saw that it was, a maverick caboose. Tipton grabbed his Johnson bar, reversing the engine, but we couldn't run backward fast enough, and the runaway smacked into us. It was so fragile that, when it hit, the darned thing fell apart on the main line in a giant cloud of dust. That was my brother-in-law's caboose. He'd left it on the round-house track to give it a scrubbing while waiting for a stock train, but as the crew were eating ham and eggs in a hash house a fierce wind came up and blew the little old hack down the line. A fast passenger train was delayed two hours while a switch engine picked up the caboose trucks."

One more runaway winds up this chapter. I remember when the Southern Pacific had a two-track wooden shed at Yuma to shelter waiting crummies from the burning heat of the Arizona sun. One track held cars of the Los Angeles Division; the other served the Tucson Division. On a very dark night, no moon or stars, a yard goat shoved a string of Tucson cabooses to the yard's east end. The first car was not coupled, which nobody seemed to notice, and it simply kept on going into the night and around a curve, and finally stopped.

Meanwhile, the switching crew made a drop of the caboose next to the engine; then they tied into the cut of cabooses and trundled them back into the yard, without bothering to count them. So the men were unaware that they had left one behind, with its crew asleep inside, out on the main line in the path of an approaching train!

Later on, one of the brakemen in that caboose woke up. Glancing out the open door, he was aghast to see that their car was not safe in the shed. Just then the long wail of an engine whistle informed him that an oncoming train had reached a milepost not far away. Grabbing a fusee from its rack, he lit it and ran excitedly down the track in bare feet and pajamas over rock ballast and dusty, splintery ties. Yes, he stopped the train in time, just barely, about three yards from the standing caboose! Afterward, when asked what had awakened him, whether some little noise or an intuition, the brakeman said solemnly it must have been his guardian angel.

I dunno. I never believed in such things but plenty of oldtimers did.

Canadian Pacific freight conductor E. V. Metcalf started a vogue on the CPR by cutting out the shape of a pig to make a thick tin overhead marker which enabled him to find his caboose easily in a busy and crowded freight yard. He followed this by making many different overhead indicators for other skippers.—NICHOLAS MORANT—CPR

NINE

Not In The Book Of Rules

DID YOU ever park your automobile in a vast parking lot
and then, hours later, forgot where you'd left it? Remember how you searched, with mounting exasperation,
among acres of vehicles vaguely like your own before finding it?
Oldtime trainmen had many comparable experiences with cabooses. Late one night, for instance, I returned to a railroad yard
after a day off, tired out and eager to hit the hay, with my crew
scheduled for an early morning call, but my home-on-wheels had
been switched several times in my absence. Reaching the spot
where I had left it, I began checking numbers, and at length found
the missing vehicle after a tedious search.

E. V. Metcalf, a Canadian Pacific freight conductor running out
of Medicine Hat, Alberta, solved such a problem by outlining a pig
on a large thick sheet of tin, cutting out the shape in a railway
shop, and then bolting it to a steel upright, roughly resembling an
aerial, and attaching the other end of the post outside his cupola.
Thereafter, in looking over a crowded railyard, he could spot his
own van quickly by seeing a pig in the air above it.

This device proved so effective that other conductors asked
Metcalf to fashion markers for their vans also, and he did, using

The caboose markers were mounted to a steel upright, resembling an aerial, and attached to the outside of the cupola. This conductor chose a Scotty dog for his van.—NICHOLAS MORANT—CPR

almost any material he could get for his handiwork. Some of his artifacts, if displayed in museums, might well evoke honorable mention as "folk art" or "modern art." Such designs by Metcalfe and others include a wide variety of shapes: animals, fish, rocking horse, clover leaf, star, circled cross, bell, horns, and so on. More than one conductor has identified his caboose with an inverted broom nailed to the rear of his sun parlor, jutting skyward. I can't say who originated this practice, but it spread to several roads and at least as far south as the Cotton Belt. Besides being a convenience for train crews, the peculiar markers have helped switchmen to find certain crummies while marking up trains.

Canadian Pacific van 43702 is, at this writing, the exclusive domain of conductor George Draper on all his runs out of the St. Luc yard. Built in 1948, it was used first by George's father, then a freight skipper; and after the older man had gone into passenger service in 1950 the van temporarily fell into disuse. George put in a bid to keep it in the family. Authorization was given. So he went to work with paint, brushes, and furnishings, and now the 43702 rolls along as a family heirloom shared in turn by father and son.

Some of Metcalf's handiwork, if displayed in museums, might well evoke honorable mention as folk art. Such designs included fish, fan blades, brooms, etc.—NICHOLAS MORANT—CPR

Some time ago a switching crew claimed that the Indiana Harbor Belt had assigned its most decrepit caboose to their industry job, designated as Calumet City No. 5. More than half the wooden siding had been ripped off, the roof tarpaper was torn and flapping, and window-panes were missing and door hinges loose. The entire top section swayed crazily while the crummy was in motion. Constant complaints to yardmasters and trainmasters had no effect; the company refused to rebuild or replace the aged relic. The unhappy crew had just about resigned themselves to the inevitable when one of them got a brainstorm. He chalked on each side of the car in letters a foot high, "The Best Caboose on the IHB," and in smaller letters beneath, "They call this featherbedding"; and wherever it rolled with these inscriptions—in Hammond, Calumet City, Burnham, and Chicago—it drew laughs. As a result the brass collars, failing to appreciate such humor, soon had the old hack repaired.

The Pennsylvania Dutch word for caboose is literally translated "little house." They have a saying, "When the little red house makes by, the train is all, ain't?"—which means, of course, that

161

the caboose marks the end of the train. Louisville & Nashville cabooses actually became little houses, and not for railroad men alone, during the Ohio River flood of 1947, when many a trainman and his family left their submerged homes to live in waycars. In those days some wives learned the fine points of cooking with skillet and pot minus the appointments of a modern kitchen. Possibly for the first time, too, long lines of family wash were strung from caboose windows to dry. After the flood ebbed people returned to their permanent homes, but it took some of the railroad men quite a while to get used to plain crummies again, without the feminine touch.

Late one stormy fall night in 1923 a Union Pacific livestock train ran into stray cattle on the track near Aikins, Kansas, killing a few and crippling others. The train stopped, of course. Two stockmen sleeping in the caboose awoke suddenly, wondering what was wrong. They heard cattle bawling on the right-of-way, saw the head brakeman take a revolver from his locker and leave without a word, and shortly afterward listened to the firing of shots. The cowboys got the impression that someone was stealing cattle from the train and they wanted to take a crack at the rustlers themselves. Wearing gun belts, they stepped off the bottom steps of the caboose, one on each side, in the rainy darkness—and fell into a stream bed 20 feet below! Although badly shocked, neither man had a bone broken, but they must have thought it was the longest step they had ever taken. Afterward, they learned that the brakeman had shot some injured steers as a humanitarian measure.

A Reading conductor was greatly embarrassed one day to see his freight train pull out of Rutherford Yard near Harrisburg, Pa., without him and his flagman. The switching crew in making up the train had inadvertently coupled on the wrong caboose. The skipper ran after the departing train, barely caught the waycar, and found it empty and padlocked. After strenuous efforts, he broke down the door to get inside, and at the first opportunity he put through a phone call for a substitute flagman.

On many Western roads the caboose track used to be a social

center for the crews away from home. Such activities usually centered around card games. Although the West had plenty of gambling joints, most railroaders preferred to play in the waycar because there was no house rake-off. Harry K. McClintock, a boomer brakeman known as "Haywire Mac," told me about the time a snow blockade had tied up 11 westbound trains in the Union Pacific yards at Laramie, Wyoming. "On that occasion," he said, "Laramie was full of men looking for diversion and I recall seeing nearly $1,000 on the caboose seat cushion that served as a gambling table."

Haywire Mac once had a regular run on the Pennsy with a partner who, like himself, was a homeless drifter. Unwilling to pay room rent for a place they'd be in for only about six days a month, they slept in the cabin car.

"The Pennsy crummies inside were painted a sickly cream color," he told me over a mug of beer, when we were reminiscing about old times, "and every finger-mark showed. We mooched enough material from the paint-shop to prime, grain, and varnish that hack until it shone like a Dutch kitchen. We painted the ceiling and cupola dark green, the walls imitation oak grain. During the intervals that our cabin stood in the yards we had window curtains and floor rugs. We painted the coalbox green and hung pictures of naked girls on the walls and had a red and yellow star on the front, and even jacked her up and oiled the springs until she rode like a buggy.

"It was a rolling palace to be proud of. Such surroundings had a good influence on us. We kept our overalls washed, and the con took to wearing a white collar. Yes, sir, our hack was the pride of the division. The trainmaster heard about it and rode over the line with us. But it was too good to last. One night my partner did a job of short flagging; an extra freight piled into us, our homelike cabin went up in smoke, my partner got fired, and I quit."

How far do cabooses wander from home rails? Sometimes pooled engines run over other railroads, but what about waycars? The Pennsy used to operate regularly a mail-express train, with a New Haven caboose on the end, that ran as far as Pittsburgh, 439 miles

Southern Pacific's caboose track at Jennings Yard, Roseville, California, can be seen through the appropriate and framing window of the Terminal Superintendent's office.—PHIL HASTINGS

from New Haven territory. It was a through Boston-Pittsburgh solid mail and express hotshot, commonly called "the fish train" because it often carried fresh fish.

Another odd Pennsy practice was running freight trains with a cabin car on *each* end between Enola yards and the Belvidere branch. Only the rear hack was occupied, but at Trenton the train would run up the branch in reverse, whereupon the other cabin was used instead of the previously-occupied one. The Belvidere hack always had a train telephone and a roof aerial, as that line was the original proving ground for such Pennsy equipment.

A few other roads also have had trains with a waycar on each end. Even today the Chesapeake & Ohio uses two cabooses on a local freight where the train's length makes the second one necessary to save time in switching. With a head-end caboose, no crew member need walk the entire train-length to reach the engine at points where switching has to be done. C&O waycars on less-than-carload-lots freight trains are usually placed near the head end to facilitate their spotting at station platforms or freight houses for partial unloading. It is desirable to have the whole crew (except the flagman) near the locomotive to assist in unloading, if necessary, without having to walk far. The same type hack is used on each end. To some extent the diesel has modified this practice on the C&O by eliminating the need for a head-end caboose on certain trains using more than one power unit and where the crew (but not the flagman) can have seats available on the engine.

At one time the Big Four system (now part of the New York Central) equipped its waycars with speed recorders known to the crews as "Dutch clocks." This device had a pencil on a moving arm that continuously marked a revolving paper disk, as long as the caboose was running, which accurately recorded train-speed and indicated where, if ever, the fixed speed was exceeded. For a while these "clocks" frustrated the engineers and conductors. Then the good word went forth. An ingenious chap in the Big Four's storeroom at East St. Louis had discovered how to outwit them. By putting a paper disk into a contraption and turning a

A near perfect reflection is cast on the waters of the Delaware River at Portland, Pennsylvania, as a Lehigh & New England freight train clatters across the long viaduct connecting Pennsylvania with New Jersey.—JOHN KRAUSE

crank you could make the disk show any speed limit you wanted and at any desired point. Thereafter, a crew that had exceeded the speed limit would donate a certain sum to the young genius; the latter would hand out a perfect speed record for that trip, and everybody was happy.

On at least one occasion, in December 1965, local members of the Brotherhood of Railroad Trainmen called a strike because of a railway's alleged failure to keep certain caboose equipment in good condition and to operate waycars on some trains. The walkout curtailed the Southern's passenger service and might have tied up the entire 10,400-mile system, but a Federal judge, gotten out of bed before a chilly dawn, issued a temporary restraining order that kept the wheels turning while the dispute was being settled.

In the early 1900's a "caboose hop"—a 4-4-0 engine and a waycar, both highly cleaned and polished—steamed out of the Burlington Railroad station at Kansas City, Missouri, with an all-Irish crew to hold religious services in remote section men's quarters and farming communities where no church was available. The crew consisted of engineer Shanahan, fireman Clancy, conductor Cassidy, and brakeman O'Flaherty. Father John Hogan, in charge of the services, later became a Bishop of the Roman Catholic diocese embracing Kansas City and St. Joseph. These were the only church services I have ever heard of in a caboose.

At Anchorage in the Union's fiftieth state railroaders built an exact replica of an Alaska Railroad caboose, scaled one inch to the foot. Mounted on runners and pulled by Eskimo dogs, it appears in street parades, ice carnivals, and other festivities and is a favorite subject for photographers. Elsewhere, a minutely detailed caboose model, fabricated to one-eighth scale by four Reading car-shop apprenticeships in about 4,000 hours of work, is on display at the company's general offices in Reading Terminal, Philadelphia. The shopmen presented it to president Sheer on his birthday, May 1, 1937, which was also the tenth anniversary of his election to a Reading vice-presidency.

A favorite subject for model railroad builders is the caboose. Actual railroad prototype plans are used and the caboose lettered for the home pike railroad. Here are scenes photographed on the Alturas & Lone Pine Railroad, a beautiful HO scale layout built by Whit Towers —president of the National Model Railroad Association.—W. TOWERS

Many model builders have built miniature waycars from standard-size plans, scaling them down; but a group of railfans living in Mt. Pleasant, Iowa, constructed a full-size, narrow-gauge caboose from blueprints for small model equipment, scaling them upward! Furthermore, they are operating it on a museum line, the Midwest Central, along with a Baldwin Mogul and other rolling stock. Another novelty is that Marshall Thayer, while spending some time in railroadless Iceland, built an HO-gauge model of this same caboose from plans based on a photograph of it.

Caboose for world's tiniest electric train is held in the palm of a young model. These postage stamp size trains are classed as N-scale and designed for apartment house pikes where space is very limited.

There was no crummy on the string of Chesapeake & Ohio hopper cars with which, day after day, conductor H. W. Doolittle of Kenney's Creek trundled coal out of the West Virginia hills and empties back to the mines. He needed a waycar urgently and said so in letters to many C&O officials. One windy, snowy, December day he lost his patience.

"I'll be danged if I can stand this much longer, riding without protection," he told his engineer. "I have asked just about everybody else on the road for a caboose and now I'm going to write to Old Man Stevens himself."

And so his cold-stiffened fingers pushed a pencil across the back of an old worksheet, composing a rhyme which he sent to George W. Stevens, president of the C&O Railway, as follows:

> I appeal to you, as man to man,
>   Kindly grant this one request
> And I promise afterward to do my best.
>   Remember now it's the 19th year
> I've decked the head end with little fear
>   Through frosty nights and days of snow,
> With weary footsteps dragging slow.
>
> I've tried my best in every way
>   To do my duty with little pay.
> I have worked G-4's and larger liz;
>   I'm almost dead with rheumatiz.
> My back is bent, my hair is gray,
>   And it's awful cold on an old slow Shay.
>
> Do try your best to give me a lift
>   By sending a caboose for a Christmas gift.
> I shall always feel grateful
>   While I work or whittle
> And be yours truly, Captain Doolittle.

Stevens responded to this atrocious doggerel by dictating a message to the division superintendent at Hinton: "Pick out the best caboose you have, not in use, and send it to Keeney's Creek for Doolittle."

The grayheaded skipper was overjoyed to get that Yuletide present, but eventually it came to an unhappy end. One spring night in 1917 he was on his regular run between Lookout and Keeney's Creek Junction when a rock and dirt slide at Nuttalburg sent the waycar toppling down the mountain side. Luckily, the crew saw it coming in time to escape. The crummy, or what is left of it, is said to be still there today, rotting and rusting in J. W. Holland's lot about 250-feet from the track. It was too far down and too much damaged to make recovery profitable.

"But that wasn't unusual," Doolittle recalled many years afterward in telling me the story. "One month in the mountains around Thurmond, West Virginia, there were 33 derailments, mostly bad ones. We got used to such things. The company made plenty of money those days hauling coal. I remember when high water damaged the Thurmond bridge so badly that it had to be condemned. I spoke to the general manager, C. E. Doyle, about the need for building a new bridge to replace it, above the old Dunglen Hotel to the east yard, which I said would be expensive. 'Doolittle,' he replied, 'judging from the amount of revenue Thurmond turns in, it would pay us even if we had to use silver piling.' Oh, yes, they built the bridge. I forgot to tell you, they gave me a new caboose right after the rock slide, and that time I didn't have to write to Old Man Stevens."

One of the seven wonders of the railroad world is the Tehachapi Loop between Bakersfield and Mojave on the San Joaquin Valley route of the Southern Pacific in Southern California. At the loop, long trains pass over themselves as they circle a cone-shaped hill.

TEN

Fact or Superstition?

NOW AND THEN I read or hear of reports of an eerie light flickering over the Atlantic Coast Line at Maco, North Carolina, 14 miles west of Wilmington. This weird glow shimmering along the rails first came to public attention one hot summer evening in 1889 when a special train bearing President Grover Gleveland stopped there to take on fuel for its woodburning 4-4-0. Cleveland, strolling down the track a few yards, saw the flagman carrying two lanterns, one red and one green, and asked why he needed both. The reply was that flagmen around Maco at night always toted two lamps to avoid being confused with "the spook light."

Back in the hazardous link-and-pin era, in 1867, tradition has it, conductor Joseph Baldwin was caught between the couplers of his caboose and the next car and was decapitated; and when, shortly afterward, the peculiar glow began to appear, men said it was Joe coming back for his head. Since then, the phenomenon has been recurring at irregular intervals.

"It seemed to be weaving directly over the tracks at a height of about five feet," said B. M. Jones, an oldtimer in the ACL's

Snow mantles Cascade, Idaho, as a Union Pacific freight performs its humble chores during zero degree temperatures.—DICK STEINHEIMER

auditing department, who claimed to have seen the light. "Then it described an arc and landed in a nearby swamp."

Those stories created such a stir that a Federal scientist was sent down from Washington to investigate. He saw the uncanny glow. "It's not a jack-o'-lantern," he told newsmen, "and it couldn't be an automobile light—it lasts too long for that, and rises and falls." But he would not say what it really was.

Later, an Army machine-gun company from Fort Bragg was assigned to summer maneuvers in and around Maco in an effort to solve the mystery. No luck! J. R. Blinn, an ACL employee, reported that a locomotive he was riding stopped for the oddity which he called "Joe Baldwin's ghost light." It's the type of thing you see on TV in *Twilight Zone*.

The death of conductor Runyon on the Wabash gave birth to another story with a hint of the supernatural. My friend Henry G. Snyder told me this one. Henry was a big hogger, tough and level-headed and not given to fantasy. He died years ago in Gulf, Mobile & Ohio service but at the time of the incident in question he was pulling Wabash freight between Kansas City and Moberly, Missouri, for a skipper named John Enzline, with the same caboose in which Runyon had been killed by a train wreck.

One night after returning from a trip and after parking the caboose in a siding, my friend and Enzline went to the beanery for corned beef and cabbage and coffee and they got talking about some queer noises like moans and groans that Enzline said he'd heard in his crummy. "It must be Runyon's ghost," he said mournfully. "I just can't sleep." Henry tried to laugh it off. "You'd better change your brand of liquor," he said. But Enzline was so serious that my friend felt sorry for the guy and offered to spend the night with him in the hack just to prove it wasn't haunted.

"And so I did," Henry told me. "We turned out the lights and lay down on bunks. At first the old waycar was quiet and peaceful and I was dozing off when I heard what sounded like a groan and a muffled shriek. I glanced across at John. 'Aw, come on,' I said. 'Cut that out!' But John denied having made any noise, and even while he was speaking I heard it again.

With the freight train safely tied down, the Sacramento Northern's car ferry *Ramon* heads across the Sacramento River. In passenger days, long green interurban trains clattered aboard the ferry on the San Francisco-Sacramento run.—W. D. MIDDLETON

"By now my curiosity was aroused. We searched that car from floor to roof, from coupler to coupler, moving everything that might possibly rub together and produce noise. Then we went outside. A bright moon was shining. We looked around for a human being, an animal, a bird, or an overhead wire that might vibrate, but nothing of the kind was in sight. We peered into the possum belly. I even got a bar and pried it for sounds, and then I pried on the steps, jumped up and down on 'em. We tried everything else we could think of, reasonable or unreasonable, but with no luck.

"After all that we lay down again and made another effort to sleep. The lugubrious sounds began anew. I stood them as long as I could. At length I got up and told John Enxline: 'This hack is all yours, brother. I'm getting outa here.' We both left and got beds in a nearby rooming-house for the rest of the night. I heard later that other crews complained so much about the same caboose that the Wabash finally dismantled it."

There must be a logical explanation for spook stories. Maybe "Joe Baldwin's ghost light" is merely a chemical emanation from the swamp, a gaseous product of radio-active disintegration that causes a pale glow. And it could be that the peculiar noises attributed to conductor Runyon's wraith were nothing more nor less than the occasional squeaks of an imperfectly-built wooden caboose-body reacting to motion or to changes in temperature as the night grew cooler. But long ago many railroad men believed in ghosts.

Caboose rides are an added attraction on many steam shortlines, including Pine Creek Railroad of the New Jersey Museum of Transportation in Allaire State Park at Farmingdale. The Pine Creek built this waycar in 1955 from old Colorado & Southern plans.—PAUL S. STEPHANUS

ELEVEN

Retired But Not Dismantled

ORDINARILY, cabooses that outlive their usefulness on the railroad are scrapped. A few become museum pieces; others are sold or donated to individuals, groups, or towns for a wide variety of uses. Aside from the Delaware & Hudson's old No. 10 the best known of all retired cabooses is the one on display at Horseshoe Curve in western Pennsylvania.

Honoring the Steam Age, the Pennsylvania Railroad keeps the last survivor of its once-great fleet of Pacific-type locomotives, class K-4s, standing like a monument on the famous Curve about five miles from the Altoona Shops which built her. Passengers can see this retired engine from the windows of passing trains. But they can't see No. 980901, the wooden-bodied Pennsy caboose that is also on exhibition at the Curve, because the cabin car—Pennsy term for caboose—stands beside the concrete highway far below track level, near the local souvenir store.

Built at Altoona in 1916, the 980901 was nicknamed "Mae West" because of the curves in its cupola. Five Pittsburgh Division veterans restored this "cabin" for display purposes. They located missing parts, repaired the old wooden structure, installed original equipment, and repainted it tuscan red, the color used in the

179

road's famous keystone emblem. For more than a century all Pennsy cabin cars were red. The latest ones, however, class N5, sport a bright orange, like the Canadian National's, for better visibility at highway crossings.

One Pennsy cabin, despite its retirement, is still active. You can ride No. 982131 on Saturdays, Sundays, and holidays behind a gas-electric locomotive up and down the mile and a half of track belonging to the Ohio Railway Museum at Worthington, a suburb of Columbus. The local chapter of the National Association of Railway Business Women bought the old cabin, had it reconditioned and repainted, and presented it to the outdoor museum. Railfans and railroad men operate this museum on a non-profit basis.

The Ohio Railway Museum at Conneaut has a Bessemer & Lake Erie caboose on exhibition; the Lima Railroad Museum in the same state has a Nickel Plate Road waycar, built by the Lafayette Car Works at Lima in 1882, and the National Museum of Transport in St. Louis boasts the Rock Island's most famous crummy, No. 18058.

Also in New York State, at Pharsalia, is caboose 95173, which covered an estimated two million miles during its 45 years of Lehigh Valley service. This antique now belongs to Charles E. Van Wormser, a retired shoe factory worker, who uses it for a souvenir store known as "Van's Little Red Caboose." If you go to Sayre, Pennsylvania, you can see four other over-age Lehigh Valley crummies which one of the road's employees acquired at the time of a housing shortage, for less than the price of a good television set, and which he rents to tenants for living quarters.

A comparable situation exists in Colorado, at Littleton. Veteran conductor N. C. Markham bought an outmoded caboose from the Denver & Rio Grande Western; but instead of using it as a fishing lodge beside the Gunnison River as he had intended, he rented it to Mrs. Jean Kounce, a widow with four children who urgently needed a place in which to live. Markham had the old vehicle parked near a school and helped the woman to make it into a comfortable home, dividing the interior into three rooms for cooking, living, and sleeping.

After 50-plus years of service, Pennsylvania Railroad cabin car 982131 was sold to the National Assn. of Railway Business Women which dolled it up and donated it to the Ohio Railway Museum at Worthington, Ohio, with the ceremony shown here.—PENNSYLVANIA RAILROAD *(Right)* A retired Baltimore & Ohio hack lowered to its last resting spot at Cumberland Park, Maryland.—BALTIMORE & OHIO

More luxurious is the Pennsy cabin-car home of Garry Moore, Jr., of Rye, New York. Imagine a stationary crummy with fine wall-to-wall carpet, knotty pine paneling, accoustic tile ceiling, nifty bathroom with shower, fireplace, gas stove, refrigerator, and gas heating. Garry bought this relic for $350 and remodeled it to provide living quarters while he attends Cornell University at Ithaca, and set it up two and a half miles from the campus.

Some retired waycars are playhouses for boys and girls. Marine Sgt. William M. Bill purchased one from the Baltimore & Ohio at scrap price, $350, and moved it from Brunswick, Maryland, to the back of his home at Libertytown in the same state, 25 miles from the nearest railroad track. Another caboose playhouse, originally No. 1438, was donated by the Santa Fe Railway to the Children's Convalescent Hospital at Bethany, Oklahoma, a suburb of Oklahoma City. Standing on the hospital lawn, it is devoted to play therapy. And in my home city of Tucson, Arizona, the SP's retired waycar 633 is displayed, thanks to the Pueblo Chapter of the National Railway Historical Society and the Arizona Pioneers' Historical Society. The 633 formerly trailed behind innumerable freight trains, work extras, and mixed consists in rain, snow, sandstorms, desert heat, and drought and even served as a guard headquarters for secret movements of United States troops during World War II.

Residents of Dutch Flat in Placer County, California, prowling in the nearby woods one day, discovered a dilapidated old caboose which they identified as having been operated long ago by a lumber company. Its owner, the Towle Estate, presented it to the village as a reminder of the fact that logging outranked mining in the area's early history. The old car, restored and standing on a section of narrow-gage track at Dutch Flat, has become a major tourist attraction.

Also in California, a caboose built by the Great Northern in 1879 and sold to the California Western in 1925, was later donated by CW's president to a retired switchman, Frank C. Heath. Standing beside Heath's home in Comptche, it is used as a museum to house red and green flags, lanterns, books of rules, train orders, switch keys, link-and pin couplers, etc. Another Californian, Warren Smith, Jr., bought a full-size Pickering Lumber Company caboose and set it up in his back yard at San Leandro to house his electically-powered miniature railroad.

Only one man that I know of ever received a real caboose as a birthday present: L. H. Gregory of Portland, Oregon, sports editor of *The Oregonian*. The caboose came from the Spokane, Portland & Seattle line, vintage of 1918. "Greg's" daughter got it for $25 and surprised her railfan father with this unique gift, complete with cupola, smokestack, cast-iron stove, hard coal in the bunker, and report forms in the conductor's desk. The new owner had it trucked down to a nearby beach for use as a summer cottage. Also in the Northwest, a farmer bought a caboose from the Potlach Forest Lumber Company, originally operated by the Washington, Idaho & Montana Railroad, and turned it into a granary on his farm near Deary, Idaho.

Down South there are many individually-owned waycars. For example, two in Georgia. Before presenting one to the Women's Club of DeSoto Park, near Rome, a division superintendent on the Southern Railway was quoted as saying: "I'll give 'em the 2828. That was old Jake Moore's crummy and I hope none of his salty language is still echoing through it. If so, there'll be some very pink female faces." Such echoes must have died out long ago, for the ladies are proud to use the caboose as a home-demonstration clubhouse, giving it a feminine touch that would have driven Jake wild. And in Athens is the caboose home of Mrs. Edith L. Stallings, dean of women at the University of Georgia. It used to be the Central of Georgia Railway's X054. Minus wheels and remodeled for modern housekeeping, with a red and gray color scheme inside and out, it boasts a kitchenette, electric stove, refrigerator, cabinet space, sleeping quarters, and a bathroom with a shower.

In Kentucky we find that Fulton's tourist information center is a former Illinois Central crummy standing between the IC tracks that stretch southward to Memphis and Birmingham, with the old marker lights still shining brightly every night; and in Louisville a banker, Hugh Staley, has a caboose which he bought from the Louisville & Nashville for $300 and on which he spent an additional $1,700 to have it moved to the back yard of his home and remodeled into a clubhouse. His wife, Nancy, uses it for bridge parties. One visitor, a retired L&N flagman, commented, "I've slept right here a thousand times in fast freight service."

By visiting the village of Boracho, Texas, you can see a string of eight cabooses transformed into motels, standing on a horseshoe-shaped track that surrounds the ninth caboose, the owner's residence. All are painted white. The proprietor, a widow, says she doesn't know which railroad they came from. And now we'll go to Arkansas. When Walter Owens retired as station agent for the Louisiana & Arkansas Railway at Stamps some years ago he announced: "A caboose is the end of a train and I am buying a caboose to symbolize the end of my railroadin' days." He had watched many a waycar flit by his depot and those memories prompted him to acquire one from the L&A and install it on his 250-acre farm, three miles south of town, to serve as a summer camp beside a lake.

Owens and his wife, a gifted artist and decorator, transformed the inside of the old hack into something no trainman would recognize. Actually a kitchenette with a lookout tower, the caboose has running water, a sink, an electric hot-plate, and a refrigerator. A midget stove doubles for cooking and heating when necessary. Storm lamps are hung on the walls for lighting while the standard caboose lights add a cheery glow. The farm is dubbed "Caboose Ranch." Whitefaced cattle graze outside the caboose and the lake offers good fishing.

At Chattanooga, the Tennessee Valley Railroad Museum exhibits waycar 41, which I may have ridden in bygone days as an L&N brakeman. This antique crummy also worked for the Florida East Coast and the Nashville, Chattanooga & St. Louis roads. The museum has 13 other pieces of railroad equipment including four full-size steam locomotives. Scores of TVRM members report for duty each week-end to scrub car interiors, paint, re-wire, and tackle other chores on the ancient rolling stock.

Possibly the only museum which displays and operates a caboose converted from a boxcar is one belonging to the 200-plus members of the Mid-Continent Railway Historical Society at North Freedom, Wisconsin. This museum carries passengers in a

Instead of being scrapped, many obsolete cabooses have been turned into homes, clubhouses, offices, playhouses for children, etc. This one, No. 114 of the now-abandoned Chestnut Ridge Railway, serves as the residence of C. W. Golden. *(Below)* This old crummy was used by the now-abandoned Laurel & Tallahoma Western as a sort of wayside freight station.—C. W. WITBECK

steam train on nine-mile tours of its own track. The museum's right-of-way was formerly an abandoned branch line bought from the Chicago & North Western, and the caboose was acquired from the Rock Island by Dr. Philip R. Hastings of Waterloo, Iowa, one of the nation's foremost railroad photographers. Dr. Hastings took possession of the waycar at Albert Lea, Minnesota, and rode in it over the C&NW to the museum at North Freedom.

The Seaboard Air Line donated an over-age waycar to a Boy Scout troop in Clinton, South Carolina, and a similar vehicle to the city itself to serve as a landmark for visitors. SAL officials estimate that the city's crummy, built in 1917 by Richmond Car Works, has logged over 2,150,000 miles. Another off-the-rails caboose was the Atlantic Coast Line's 50186 that Walter Hawkins, Jr., of Jacksonville bought and placed outside his fruit-packing plant in Florida on U.S. Highway 1 as a memorial to his father, who was a pioneer railroader in that state. The car is a museum displaying railroad pictures, old letters, passes, and other railroadiana. It stands on rails, retaining its trucks and air-brake rigging.

Another ex-ACL caboose in Florida, No. 0408, rests on a 40-foot track in Crandon Park on Key Biscayne, with a railroad museum built around it. This final and prominent resting place was reached after a four-year legal battle that stretched as far as the State Supreme Court. And just to make sure the small red waycar wouldn't feel lonely, the Dade County Park Department placed it only a few feet from Key Biscayne's sole operating railroad, the narrow-gauge Biscayne Bay, Atlantic & Gulf tourist attraction which takes passengers on a mile-and-a-half tour of the park.

The controversy began in 1960 when William M. Phillips, a newspaper feature editor, bought the 0408 from the Atlantic Coast Line for $750, paid an additional $500 to move it from Waycross, Georgia, to his home, and installed it in his back yard as a playhouse for his three children, on a hurricane-proof foundation that set him back $1,000. Neighbors complained that this installation violated the local zoning code. A long round of lawsuits and county hearings began. At one time Phillips was permitted to retain the caboose if he'd paint it green and screen it from public view with foliage. This he did, but the ruling was later overturned.

There's lots of personal history in retired Burlington caboose 14209 shown with its owner, Arthur Gordon. In 1899, Gordon was promoted to conductor and assigned this caboose. While releasing a stuck air-brake in 1905, he fell under the train and lost a foot. In 1961 he bought his old crummy and set it up in his backyard at Merna, Nebraska.—TELEGRAPH-BULLETIN, NORTH PLATTE, NEBRASKA (Below) Unlike the hobbyist who built his model from real railroad plans, this full-size hack was constructed from scale model plans.—MARSHALL THAYER

After losing his last appeal in 1964, the journalist reluctantly donated his caboose to the park. Together with the legal expenses, he said, it had cost him about $5,000.

"I wish now that I had just built a little house for the children," he added, "instead of buying a caboose."

The old car was repainted its original color and turned into a museum housing oilburning lanterns, waybills (some dating back to the 1880's), historical photographs, and other railroad material from collector Seth Bramson.

But no zoning law disturbed John C. Jay, a bank cashier, in his proud ownership of a back-yard caboose museum at Greensboro, Alabama. The erstwhile Southern Railway crummy X-2260 squats on a cinder-block base instead of wheels and truck. By day its red paint gleams brightly and at night its electrified marker lights cast crimson and amber reflections across the dark lawn. The cozily furnished and well polished interior houses part of Jay's 30-year collection of railroadiana. Framed pictures adorn the walls. Telegraph instruments, lanterns, spikes, signal flags, scrapbooks, and so on line the shelves. Engineers' peaked hats hang from pegs in neat rows.

After a time, Jay laid 85-feet of track from his home to the caboose, and his outdoor show took on a handcar, an antique track velocipede, a rail motorcar, tall semaphore poles, maintenance limit markers, and a milepost sign. People from almost every state in the Union as well as Canada and some countries overseas have visited "Jay's Caboose." Upon returning home, many of them sent him additional museum pieces. The number of relics increased to such an extent that, at his request, the Southern Railway donated a second caboose to hold them. It arrived after his death, but his widow is using it to display the hundreds of fresh items.

"I helped John quite a lot on the first caboose," she told me, "and I'll continue this work as a memorial to him."

This 3-foot gauge caboose on the Santa Fe & Disneyland Railroad has run 200,000 miles since it was constructed. Seats in the cupola are quickly filled with juveniles as the train makes its way around the famous park at Anaheim, California.—GERALD M. BEST *(Below)* This old Atlantic Coast Line way car forms part of the train that regularly runs over the shortline of the Gold Coast Railroad of the Miami Railroad Historical Society in Florida.—JAMES G. LA VAKE

Western Pacific's modern bay window caboose No. 432 ducks under
the head end of its own eastbound freight train at Williams Loop, on
the main line between Keddie and Portola, California.—DICK STEIN-
HEIMER

TWELVE

Efficient But Not Homelike

THE WOODEN-BODIED red caboose, famed in song and story for a hundred years, is fast becoming as rare as a horse-car on city streets. Modern cabooses, impersonal but efficient, are built of steel, some with aluminum roofs, and usually equipped with stainless-steel and electronic appliances. Relatively few are painted red. The New York Central's are green, the Baltimore & Ohio's blue and gold, the Pennsy's and Canadian National's a bright orange, the Louisville & Nashville's gray with yellow trim, and so on.

Each road has its own specific requirements for the cabooses it is building or buying, but those on the Northern Pacific are fairly typical of modern trends. Let's examine a batch of NP waycars from the International Car Corporation of Buffalo, New York, the nation's largest builder of cabooses. Built almost entirely of welded steel, the exceptions being the plywood lining and the floor, they are equipped with a steel "grab bar" which extends along the ceiling center of the car, safety window glass, seat belts in the cupola, flush toilets, and electric lights throughout, including track lights, markers, and step signal lights. Corners on the lockers, handrails, etc., are rounded to help reduce injuries from slack

Some modern cabooses are built with safety treads on platforms and steps. *(Below)* This present-day Monon caboose looks almost like a hospital ward. The electric refrigerator and stove are vastly different from the furnishings in the crummies the author rode.

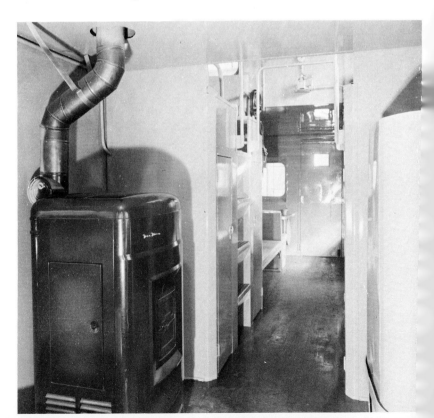

action. Anti-slip steel treads are used on running boards, platforms, and steps, to insure safer footing.

The traditional round-bellied stove, which was usually topped with a cooking pot and a percolator, has given way to an oilburning space heater and, for cooking, a propane-fired two-burner stove. A cabinet unit, of which the stove is a part, also contains a gas-operated refrigerator with a built-in water cooler and a sink. An overhead tank supplies water by gravity to the sink and cooler.

Each caboose is further equipped with two high-backed, leather-covered, foam-filled conductor's chairs at desks in front and rear. Large thermopane observation windows above the desks provide ample daylight illumination. Two-channel radios, including loudspeakers, are installed at each end of the desks, while a third set hangs on a wall between the two cupola sets. This represents an advance from radio equipment used in earlier installations, the modifications due to the increased size of cabooses and the necessity of providing electricity for lighting and a blower. The NP's communications department designed these developments.

Less apparent, but surely a major improvement, is a new cushioned underframe which reduces the impacts of starting and stopping the train. Swing-motion trucks provide passenger-car qualities. As trainmen say, "She rides like a cradle." The old wooden crummies were all right when they were new, but you can't beat steel for wear after your hack has been highballing behind fast freights for a few years. Then you can tell whether or not there's a good solid car under you. Today's cabooses are built to stand up under the hardest wear, particularly in service where pusher engines are used.

The Northern Pacific's new cabooses have the conventional cupola, located midway on the roof, but the modern trend elsewhere is to eliminate the cupola. Without a cupola, there is no need for partitions inside the car. This makes a roomier, more airy, and more readily heated vehicle. Some roads abandoned the cupola as long ago as 1937, on the ground that the height of jumbo boxcars impaired the trainman's view of his train. Instead, they use protruding bay windows at floor level on both sides of the caboose, the reason being that a man seated in a bay window can inspect his train more effectively and detect hotboxes (overheated

The Erie-Lackawanna freight train conductor, whose signals from the caboose may not be immediately seen when the train is rounding a curve or traveling at night or in foggy weather, can instantly be in contact with the engineer, dispatcher, or the nearest way station without leaving his seat in the cupola.—ERIE-LACKAWANNA

The Delaware & Hudson uses portable Motorola radio-telephones as the modern means of communication between engineer-conductor-dispatcher. In these scenes, the conductor of a titanium ore train in the heart of the Adirondacks calls for a clear track.—JIM SHAUGHNESSY

journals) more readily, as odors hang close to the ground. Besides there is the safety factor of no longer a need for scaling a ladde into the cupola. Some bay windows are even equipped with wind shield wipers.

The Monon Railroad broke an old tradition by moving its bay windows upstairs. That is to say, it incorporates bay windows inte the cupola itself, one on each side extending out nine inches. Each side of the bay has two sliding windows, with a fixed window at the center and two stationary windows at each side. All glass i one-quarter-inch safety plate, with no sash. The outside sheet o the caboose body and cupola is cut out for windows. Edge surface are ground smooth and the glass is set in a foam-rubber sea section. Several other roads also have "upstairs" bay windows, a idea which the Duluth, Missabe & Iron Range claims to have originated.

All four corner posts of the Monon's cupolas are continuous o the Z-bar side posts, thus making the cupola an integral part of the car body. Four diagonal braces on each side at the car's center add strength and rigidity. Two H-beam collision posts at each end ar spaced to form the door posts. All windows except four sliding one in the cupola are stationary.

Each of these Monon cabooses has three bunks and two end seats with desks. Seat and bunk cushions are foam rubber covered with a tan fabric-backed plastic. Water is supplied by a 200-gallon tank, which also has an outside access for emergency use i hotboxes develop. The car is equipped with type E long-shank couplers, six-inch rubber draft gears, Waughmat truck side bear ings, and Ajax hand-brakes. A radio unit consisting of a rack mounted transmitter, a receiver, and 12-volt DC power supply permits the conductor and rear brakeman to communicate with the head end, wayside stations, and train dispatchers. There is also a walkie-talkie unit.

Shortly after the radio-telephone system was installed in Erie cabooses, a wayside operator noticed two men who appeared to be fugitives hiding between cars on a passing freight. He surmised correctly that they were two escaped convicts he had heard about so he called the state police and directed them to a crossing. Then he radioed the conductor to stop the train at the crossing, with the

As the world's largest independent caboose builder, the International Car Corporation, Buffalo, New York, has designed and erected some of the most distinctive way cars. Based on superiority of construction, emphasis on safety, operating efficiency and crew comfort, the modern railroad looks to the specialist for their cabooses. In these scenes, a modern Monon caboose under construction and on the ready track.

FLOOR PLANS

... here are a few of the many International Caboose Car floor plans ...

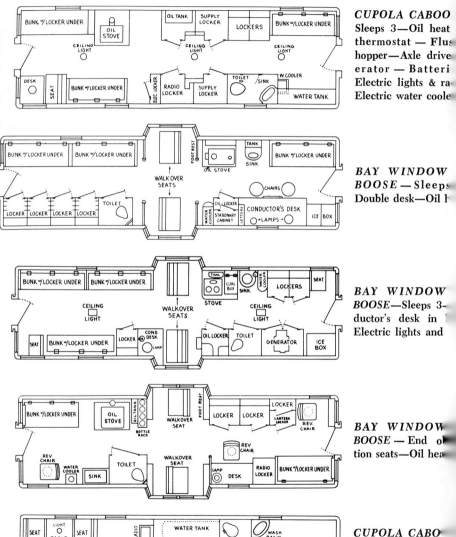

CUPOLA CABOO...
Sleeps 3—Oil heat
thermostat — Flus
hopper—Axle drive
erator — Batteri
Electric lights & ra
Electric water coole

**BAY WINDOW
BOOSE** — Sleeps
Double desk—Oil h

**BAY WINDOW
BOOSE**—Sleeps 3-
ductor's desk in
Electric lights and

**BAY WINDOW
BOOSE** — End o
tion seats—Oil hea

CUPOLA CABO...
Flushing hopper—
generator — E
water cooler—E
lights and radio.

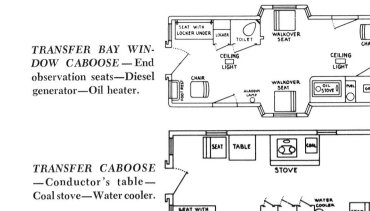

TRANSFER BAY WINDOW CABOOSE — End observation seats—Diesel generator—Oil heater.

TRANSFER CABOOSE —Conductor's table— Coal stove—Water cooler.

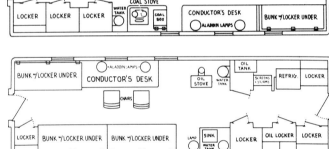

CUPOLA CABOOSE— Sleeps 3 — Cabinet sink —Double desk—Cupola near end of car.

CUPOLA CABOOSE— Sleeps 4 — Chemical toilet—Hot and cold water — Cabinet sink — Diesel generator.

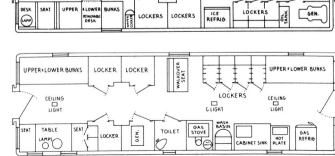

CUPOLA CABOOSE— Sleeps 3 — Cabinet sink —Oil heater—Double desk —Cupola near end of car.

CUPOLA CABOOSE— Sleeps 4—Propane stove —Hot plate and refrigerator—Propane generator —Flushing hopper— Electric lights.

cars in question spanning the road. As the train stopped, the police grabbed the stowaways.

On some cabooses electricity comes from a diesel power plant and on others from axle-driven equipment. This supplies current for such needs as a mechanical refrigerator, a two-burner cook stove, electric fans, interior lighting, and marker lamps. The New York Central's new and modernized cabooses do not have the traditional exterior oil-lamp markers but use electric lamps on each of the four exterior corner posts. Many waycars today are heated by a duotherm space heater drawing its fuel from a 30-gallon tank. Its thermostat is easily set by train crews.

Back in the early '90's when I began railroading nearly all caboose stoves were coalburners. Today they burn oil, coal, electricity, or propane gas. The last-named is becoming increasingly popular because of its features of clean burning, quiet operation, and convenience of storage cylinders. Three cylinders of gas are contained in each car, and one filling is enough for about 50 hours of normal service operation.

Thus we see that the modern steel caboose is a rolling collection of the very latest ideas intended to make it pleasant and safe for trainmen. To avoid bruises and snagged clothing, all hardware is flush, including the steps to the cupola. Geared power hand-brakes have replaced the manual-type brakes. Instead of wood, the floors on many new cabooses are covered with abrasive, non-slip, sanitary material.

"One big innovation," writes M. A. Nugent, the Southern Pacific's superintendent of safety, "is our new type of draft gear that permits drawbar travel, yet the slack action is minimized to the men in the caboose. I am proud of my part in the adoption of shatter-proof glass throughout the caboose, which we started in 1954. In many areas along our lines, as on other railroads, youngsters throw rocks at trains and shoot BB guns with trainmen as a prime target. Prior to the adoption of safety glass we had many injuries from those sources."

Safety is, indeed, the keynote in modern caboosing. On the Elgin, Joliet & Eastern, for example, the front and back platforms and steps are built of open gratings so that no snow, ice, rain or mud is likely to accumulate there. Below the markers, on the

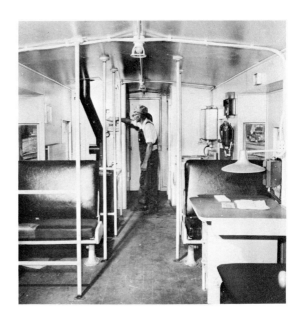

All modern cabooses are steel-built. Many like this Milwaukee Road car have no cupola, but do have a bay window on each side and radio-telephones. A diesel plant supplies electric power to refrigerator, cook stove, and interior lighting.—MILWAUKEE ROAD *(Below)* Kitchen, locker and breakfast nook of a Chicago & Illinois Midland way car.

In the days when steam was king on Southern Pacific rails, a slow freight kicks up a smoke storm while California's mighty Mount Shasta looks on.—GUY L. DUNSCOMB

outside end of the caboose, two squares of red Scotchlite gleam brightly in the darkness when a light of any kind is played on them. Inside, the steps leading to the cupola are recessed into the walls and do not protrude into the aisle. "J" cabooses also have non-spin hand-brakes.

For originating the use of safety belts in the cupola the Duluth, Missabe & Iron Range received the National Safety Council's award of honor for public safety activities. Several roads have since adopted this innovation. An instance of its usefulness occurred one August day in 1964. A Union Railroad crew was making a routine run with an ore train through East Pittsburgh, Pennsylvania, when the caboose coupler-key dropped out and the coupler fell from the buffer casting to the middle of the track. The caboose, now separated from the train, hit the coupler, derailing the forward truck, and traveled three car-lengths before stopping. Seated in the cupola at the time were conductor I. W. Harris and brakeman H. R. Wadsworth, both wearing safety belts. Neither man was hurt by the violent jolt, but without those belts they almost certainly would have been hurled to the floor.

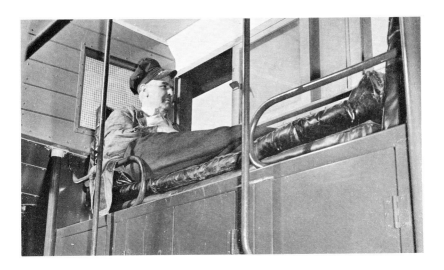

New Haven trainman leisurely watches the scenery roll by from the crow's nest of his waycar.—NEW HAVEN RAILROAD

At Cos Cob, Connecticut, Jim Shaughnessy photographed this caboose on the tag end of a New Haven piggyback train running between New York and Boston via the Shore Line.

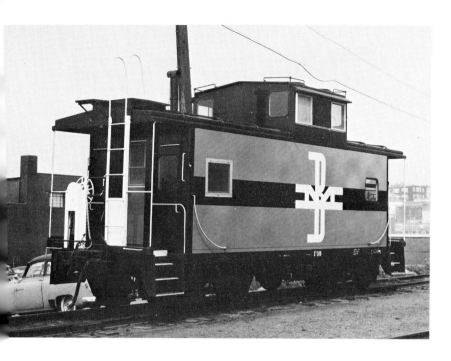

The red caboose is fast becoming as rare as the old steam locomotive. The modern caboose is more colorful, safer, better constructed and more comfortable. In the view above, a new Boston & Maine caboose complete with ornamental monogram.—BOSTON & MAINE *(Below)* A silver and orange Rio Grande crummy rolls west through Funston Yard at Glenwood Springs, Colorado.—EVERETT L. DE GOLYER, JR.

Some northern roads, including the White Pass & Yukon Route, use steel cabooses with no *front* platform, eliminating it from the design so that the car could be assigned to rotary plows without having that platform plugged with snow or ice while the crew is bucking heavy drifts. The *rear* platform, however, is of standard construction and the caboose is usually equipped at the rear with a standard locomotive headlight and flangers. Another development in recent years—on the Bangor & Aroostook, the Missouri Pacific, and a few other roads—is the return of the side-door caboose, which for many years had been regarded as hazardous.

Instead of the hard bunk, the smoky stove, and (sometimes) the bucket of icewater that I well remember, the new shiny cabooses on railroads all over the United States and Canada have luxurious foam-rubber or curled-hair mattresses which can be made into beds, and cupola seats built on couches, if cupolas are used, and a sleek, roomy refrigerator, and running water, including flush toilets. The conductor's desk is equipped with a cushioning pad along its edge to protect him from bruises in case of sudden stops. In fact, special rubber equipment on the new cars minimizes the jolts and jerks due to take-up of slack in a long train. Many cabooses have three-inch insulation in the roofs, sides, and ends and even two inches of cork in the floor to provide additional warmth in winter as well as coolness in summer. (What, no air-conditioning?) These cars are about as efficient and homelike as the Empire State Building. Trainmen can keep them clean with a little soap and elbow grease.

Along with the modernization of cabooses has come the pooling system. Instead of assigning a car to a certain conductor for an indefinite period, for him to work and live in maybe for years, the railroads, one after another, have turned to pooling the cabooses and assigning them for single runs or round trips. This system is being adopted under agreements made with the Brotherhood of Railroad Trainmen and the Order of Railway Conductors and Brakemen.

The roads no longer switch waycars merely because the train crews are changed. Take the Rock Island, for example. Formerly both the caboose and the crews were changed at Caldwell and Waurika, Kansas, but now the caboose stays in the train at these

Burlington's 1964-built way cars came in two most distinct cupola designs. In the view above, the sleek *Zephyr* style, while below the odd "saddlebag" type cupola. Both designs are painted the familiar Burlington aluminum color with red Scotchlite striping. Emblems, also Scotchlite, are white on black with a red border.—JIM C. SEACREST

This National Railways of Mexico freight photographed near Teo-calco, resembles many U.S.A. roads.—MICHAEL A. EAGLESON

points but fresh crews are taken on. This means, among other things, that the crummy is no longer the lodging place of crews going off duty. The men pick up their belongings—which they formerly stored in caboose lockers—and spend the night in a hotel or boarding house, the railroad paying for their rooms. Further-more, locker space for their clothing and other possessions is provided in buildings at points where crews are changed.

But despite the pooling system, the railroads are hauling such a heavy volume of freight traffic at this writing that some of them are running out of cabooses. The Burlington, for one, is bringing old commuter passenger cars out of retirement, fitting them with conductors' desk, and pressing them into service as cabooses on branch-line freight runs.

Previously, train crews were responsible for the care of their cabooses, supplying the stoves with coal and keeping their quarters, including toilets, clean. Now the railroads are doing it—

every road which has adopted the new setup. This system expedites the movement of trains, thus providing the shippers with more efficient service, and cuts the company's overhead expenses, even though it pays for rooms, lockers, and so on. As a rule $2 is paid to each man for whom suitable lodgings cannot be provided. Conductors and trainmen not covered by pooled caboose agreements receive $2.50 instead of $2. The agreements usually provide also that pool-freight conductors and trainmen using pooled waycars are paid an allowance of one cent for each road mile actually run, with a minimum payment of $1, which applies only once between the initial and final payments.

No longer will you find cabooses with lace curtains, linoleum or carpet on the floor, lithographs and photographs on the walls, stoves with miniature "fences" around the top to prevent cooking utensils from being jolted to the floor, nor the lingering aromas of fried bacon, coffee, and tobacco blended into a pleasant whole. Even the cigar boxes with one end removed have disappeared; the papers that once stuffed 'em are now in the skipper's brief case or neatly filed in some cabinet.

Altoona shops of the Pennsylvania Railroad built many of these semi-streamlined cabooses with porthole windows. — MICHAEL A. EAGLESON

After a rolling inspection of a passing Southern Pacific train, Bill
Black gives a fellow conductor an "all okey" signal.—ED CARROLL

When cabooses are pooled, crews no longer have a personal interest in them. A crew that rides over a division on a certain waycar may not see that same car again for six months. So why should they decorate or fix it for any further use? As for creature comforts, the modern steel caboose has the old wooden version skinned by a country mile. G. H. Harris, past president of the ORC&B, puts it this way:

"Truly an era has been passing from the railroad scene as more and more of our organizations' representatives agree in negotiations with the railroads to replace the old assigned caboose, that was regarded almost as the conductor's property, with the pooled caboose, either newly built or completely remodeled with modern conveniences, even luxuries.

"Progress, of course, cannot be stopped. The changes being made in the caboose as it moves from the kerosene-light era to the age of electric lights and two-way radio represent only one example of the revolution taking place in every aspect of railroading. The modern computer is certainly bearing down on the carriers. This is inevitable, due largely to the need to meet competition. However, it does relegate to years past the glorious age when the pace was more leisurely and when the conductors and brakemen were more closely knit through their 'palace on wheels' and 'home away from home.'"

All this takes my mind back to a Southern Pacific trip many years ago. My caboose was a simple boxcar with wooden ladders, nails beside the sliding door, marker brackets nailed to the corners of the desk, an inverted box with four strips of wood for legs, crude wooden bunks stuck in the corners, and no stove. That run handled the first pre-cooled refrigerator cars sent out of California, so naturally it was a high-speed run. We had but eight cars and that caboose. My brakeman and I bounced around like peas on a hot skillet. I tried to write my wheel report but the desk would move away in one direction and the chair, including me, in another. Finally I solved that problem by tieing the legs of the desk to the chair with two handkerchiefs, my own and the brakeman's. That was a trip I shall always remember.

The tottering caboose operated by Utah's Tooele Valley Railway, complete with crooked smokestack, resembles the famous creation of Fontaine Fox—the Tooonerville Trolley. In this scene, the daily freight nears the city of Tooele.—DICK STEINHEIMER

THIRTEEN

Caboose Gallery

THE sightseeing upper deck of Vista Dome passenger cars is said to have been adapted from the caboose cupola, which only goes to show how many angles there are, pictorial and otherwise, to the caboose business. I'd need two or three books to cover all the variations and oddities, all the off-beat types and occasional uses of this vehicle, from the old wooden four-wheelers to the modern steel indestructibles. Take tombstones, for example. Stone likenesses of waycars mark at least three rail-roaders' graves. A Gulf, Mobile & Ohio conductor, Kellie C. Riley (1878-1948), is buried at Columbus, Mississippi, below the outline of his eight-wheeled X-155 cut deeply into a flat granite slab. In the same cemetery is a similar marker for his son John, also a GM&O skipper, who survived him only one year. And at Uhrichs-ville, Ohio, B&O conductor Charles E. Witting, who died May 4, 1900, at age 27, sleeps out eternity underneath a five-foot-high stone model of his four-wheeled waycar. He wanted it that way. As I said, caboose lore is endless. I saved this last chapter for a variety of pictures that didn't seem to fit anywhere else, but it would take many, many more pages to tell the entire story of crummies.

Unusual Cabooses

There is probably more individuality in the railroad caboose than any other type of rolling stock, and of course this goes double for the short line. The only uniform feature and universal attribute of crummies are round wheels, air brakes, automatic couplers and a variable degree of availability to human occupancy. Everything else is the product of necessity, environment or whim, including their size, shape, frequency of windows, number of doors, presence of porches, cupolas and other architectural embellishments. Here is a rather interesting selection of unusual wood and steel cabooses.

GRAFTON & UPTON No. 3—Box like homemade steel caboose which barely covers the pair of trucks. Note the lack of cupola.—GERALD M. BEST COLLECTION

PIEDMONT & NORTHERN X-23—Modern steel caboose with airplane styled propeller on the roof which drives a generator inside hack.—GERALD M. BEST COLLECTION

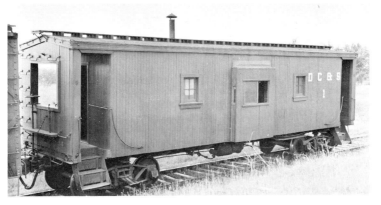

DETROIT, CAIRO & SANDUSKY No. 1 — Built with wooden bay window on the side and picture window veranda on each end.—
GERALD M. BEST COLLECTION

NEW ORLEANS & LOWER COAST RAILROAD No. 2618 — Unique side-door caboose used in the Louisiana delta country. —
GERALD M. BEST COLLECTION

SOUTHERN PACIFIC No. 902—Unique "shelter car caboose" used for transfer runs in and around Taylor Yard, Los Angeles, California.
—GERALD M. BEST

LOUISVILLE, NEW ALBANY & CORYDON No. 1942—This hack complete with awnings has a center cupola with leaning sides.—
GERALD M. BEST COLLECTION

PETALUMA & SANTA ROSA No. 07—Unusually high cupola with roof access doors was the rule on this California interurban line.—
G. M. BEST COLLECTION

OUACHITA & NORTH WESTERN No. 505—There appears to be a little tudor influence in the cupola architecture of this caboose.—
GERALD M. BEST COLLECTION

Unusual Cupolas

Webster's *International Dictionary* defines the word cupola as, "An observation post in the roof of a railroad caboose used by brakemen to keep watch over a train while it is in motion." A great deal of variety has been shown in the placement of the cupola. You can find it anywhere from the extreme end to the exact middle—according to the designer. Cupola shape and complexion, the contour of its facade and elevation, the frequency of windows and clerestories depend on the railroad. Today many of the most modern cabooses, like the earlier ones, do not have cupolas. This pictorial gathering covers just about every type in the design book.

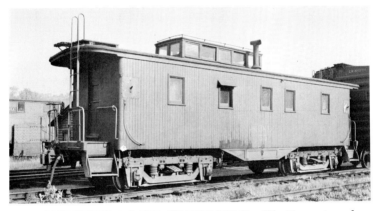

ST. JOHNSBURY & LAKE CHAMPLAIN No. 55—Vermont made caboose-coach with highspeed trucks and large center clerestory section.—G. M. BEST COLLECTION

KANSAS CITY SOUTHERN No. 503—Classic cupola with indicator lantern on top. Note the fine riding passenger car trucks.—GERALD M. BEST COLLECTION

Wood Caboose Classics

There is more warmth of homeliness and sentiment about a wooden caboose at the end of a string of high cars than the gaudy steel hack. It is a little self-contained world of creaky joints, windows that won't open, and vents sawed in to suit the occupant. Over in the corner sits the cannonball stove installed in a sandbox to keep from burning a hole in the floor. The wood caboose followed the converted boxcar; since side door entry caused the loss of so many lives it became a menace and outlawed in many states. The curved grabiron which helps swing a know-how brakeman up the step of a moving string of cars came with the modern wood hack. Other innovations included steel underframes, platforms, steps and ladders. Before long the caboose was made entirely of steel.

ARCADE & ATTICA No. 303—The caboose on this 15-mile New York line is both a rolling Railway Express Agency and U.S. Post Office.—G. M. BEST COLLECTION

GREAT WESTERN No. 1008—Extra braces hold down the cupola on this wood beauty which rolls on Colorado's prime sugar beet carrier.—G. M. BEST

MAGMA ARIZONA RAILROAD No. 101—The characteristic red way car with black trim still rolls on this 100 per cent steam short line.—G. M. BEST

ROCK ISLAND No. 18039—This cupola caboose with passenger car trucks, is a fine example of wood classics used on the main line.— G. M. BEST

APALACHICOLA NORTHERN X-7—This hack with passenger car trucks, makes the daily 96-mile run on Florida's *St. Joe Route.*—G. M. BEST COLLECTION

SANTA FE No. 915—Operated in California's San Joaquin Valley during the war era. Roof seats were used for passing signals while switching.—AL ROSE

MERIDIAN & BIGBEE RIVER No. 104—This deep South waycar has two side doors and a ladder to the roof for quick signal passing. —G. M. BEST COLLECTION

LAKE SUPERIOR TERMINAL & TRANSFER No. 04—The hack on this Wisconsin switching road has side and end sill doors and small bay window.—G. M. BEST COLLECTION

Cabooses From Boxcars

The railroad caboose has two properties in common with every other way car: it rolls on wheels in trains obedient to the rails; and it provides a refuge from the elements. Around the turn of the century, the converted boxcar with doors at the end or sliding doors on the side was commonplace. The boxcar caboose rapidly disappeared in the early 1900's, only to return again during World War I and II, when new equipment was scarce. Modern way cars with cupolas, heaters, electric lights, or radio-telephones, seldom find their way to branch or short lines, whose coffers run dry more often than main line carriers. This gallery of boxcar cabooses covers the war years on the main line and those used on the short line during the past 20 years.

MISSISSIPPI CENTRAL B-19—Novel way car on Mississippi's *Natchez Route* has end doors and a sliding door in the center.—G. M. BEST COLLECTION

SOUTHERN PACIFIC No. 22824—Remodeled boxcar converted into a caboose in 1941. Used primarily for switching runs around Los Angeles.—G. M. BEST

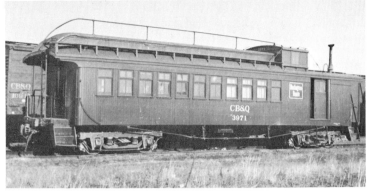

BURLINGTON ROUTE No. 3971—Caboose-coach rebuilt from an old passenger car for use on branch lines around Lincoln, Nebraska. —JIM SEACREST COLLECTION

MIDLAND CONTINENTAL No. 707—This North Dakota shortline still offers caboose passenger service according to the Official Guide. —G. M. BEST COLLECTION

SANTA FE RAILWAY D947—This odd looking transfer coach caboose is used in Chicago's Corwith Yard to transport crews in freight trains.—H. REID

Caboose Coaches

The number of railroads on which passengers are permitted to ride the caboose is comparatively small, but there are still more of these runs in existence than may be imagined by the casual travelling public. The caboose-coach was designed primarily to haul miners or lumberjacks to a particular location, however the public was invited. Some roads substituted the caboose-coach idea as a replacement when the doodlebug could not justify its expense. On some branch lines the caboose-coach might carry the local express, mail or peeping chickens to the feed store. On the Tucson, Cornelia & Gila Bend in the Arizona desert, the caboose-coach sports a footstool, while the Rock Island Southern accommodates passengers in the crummy as a regular thing.

McCLOUD RIVER No. 03—This beautiful caboose-coach with two whistles on its cupola was used to haul lumberjacks to logging camps.
—GUY L. DUNSCOMB

VIRGINIA & TRUCKEE No. 10—This bright yellow caboose-coach with passenger trucks was used to carry miners on freight trains.—
G. M. BEST

Narrow Gauge Cabooses

Because of its unique status in the roster of railroad equipment, the narrow gauge caboose achieved an individuality unshared by the standard gauge models. Their diminutive dimensions held a peculiar and warming enchantment in the collective mind of a nation dedicated to doing everything on the biggest and best scale imaginable. In 1871, the Denver & Rio Grande received designs for a 3-foot gauge caboose for their line under construction. Before long, the narrow gauge, like so many other evidences and manifestations of individualist enterprise, succumbed to a level of standardization for the narrow gauge hack. Here are five smartly designed narrow gauge cabooses photographed during the last 30 year period—end of the narrow gauge era.

OAHU RAILWAY C1—This Hawaiian narrow gauge caboose is one of the few ever built without a window in the body section.—G. M. BEST

SANDY RIVER & RANGELEY LAKES No. 551—Caboose-coach with clerestory cupola, once the pride of this Maine two-footer.— G. M. BEST COLLECTION

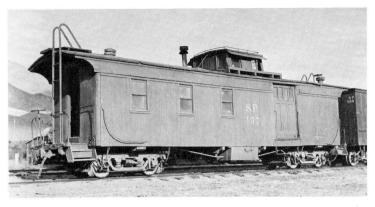

SOUTHERN PACIFIC No. 467—Caboose-coach built at Central Pacific shops for the Carson & Colorado. Once had twice as many windows.—G. M. BEST

EDAVILLE RAILROAD No. 557—Former Sandy River and Rangeley Lakes caboose now operating on this Massachusetts Cranberry pike.—G. M. BEST COLLECTION

PACIFIC COAST RAILWAY No. 2—When acquired from the Nevada-California-Oregon this caboose was equipped with a side door.—G. M. BEST COLLECTION

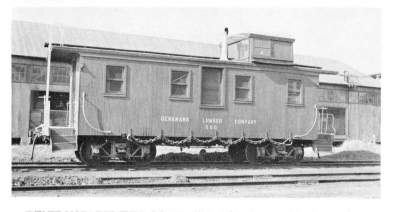

DENKMANN LUMBER CO. No. 500—This Canton, Mississippi, log carrier purchased its shack second hand. Note emergency chains.—
G. M. BEST COLLECTION

RAYONIER INCORPORATED—A wood shanty mounted on a steel flat car is a caboose on this Washington state logging carrier.—
DONALD DUKE

ANGELINA COUNTY LUMBER CO. No. 2—Loggers call a caboose a "shelter car" if it has long supply platforms on each end.—GERALD M. BEST COLLECTLON

Logging Cabooses

The function of the logging railroad caboose was to provide a place for the train crew to ride and a vantage point from which to watch for shifting or falling logs, derailments or a hot box. In the early days of rail logging, most log trains did not carry cabooses, the crews merely rode the engine. As the cab became too crowded, a shed was skidded onto a flat car during the winter months. Over the years most logging cabooses were nothing more than homemade products designed to resemble a regular caboose. Flush logging pikes purchased used wood hacks from a main line carrier, and a few went so far as to buy them new. The logging shanty was a breed of cats to itself as you can see in this gallery covering western and southern rail logging carriers.

WEST SIDE LUMBER CO. No. 1—California's erstwhile narrow gauge logger built its own cabooses in their Tuolumne shops.—
G. M. BEST

CLOVER VALLEY LUMBER CO. No. 99—This northern California logger obtained their bright red caboose from the Western Pacific.—
GUY L. DUNSCOMB

Four-Wheel Cabooses

The four-wheel caboose came into being by the imaginings and necessities of finger shy link 'n pin brakemen and freight conductors who required some sort of shelter from the storm in which to light their lanterns and tally waybills. You might say the four-wheel bouncer was the first type of American caboose, a condensed version of the larger hack without sleeping accommodations. The four-wheeler was popular for daylight service and short runs. It took up less space, was lighter to haul and could navigate the tightest curve. As an example of its utility, the New York, Ontario & Western had 106 four-wheel and 60 eight-wheel cabooses on its roster during its prime years. These little four-wheel hacks came in all sizes and shapes, with or without cupola, and nearly every road had one of these valiant little shacks on its roster at one time or another.

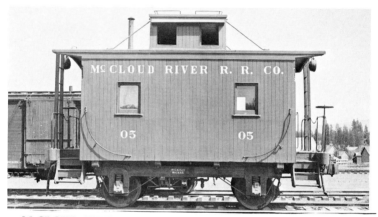

McCLOUD RIVER No. 05—This California common carrier used four-wheel hacks for crew quarters on the end of its log trains.—GUY L. DUNSCOMB

CUMBERLAND & PENNSYLVANIA No. 143—Smartly designed and handsomely painted hack displaying the road's herald on the rear platform.—G. M. BEST COLLECTION

THE BELT RAILWAY OF CHICAGO No. 30—This colorful shack boasts a novel bay window in place of the usual roof clerestory.—
G. M. BEST COLLECTION

MORRISTOWN & ERIE No. 1—This caboose is the delight of its crew even though it seldom travels more than 20 miles in a day.—
G. M. BEST COLLECTION

COLORADO & SOUTHERN No. 1009—This narrow gauge bouncer once rolled to Black Hawk and Idaho Springs in Colorado's lusty youth.—G. M. BEST

BURLINGTON ROUTE No. 13554—This stylish all-steel car is painted aluminum color making it ten per cent cooler in summer.—G. M. BEST

CITY OF PRINEVILLE No. 202—Modern bay window caboose with express section as operated by this 19-mile Oregon short line.—G. M. BEST COLLECTION

NORFOLK & WESTERN No. 562838 — Former Wabash super de-luxe hack now carries the familiar Norfolk & Western herald on its side.—F. W. TRITTENBACH

Modern Steel Cabooses

Once they were called "crummies." Nowadays, they're everything but crummy. In fact many can be called parlor cars with all the conveniences and comforts that are being packed into their all steel construction body. Today's hacks with their bay windows of shatterproof glass, automatic oil heater, electric lights and refrigerator, drinking fountain, radio-telephone and specially designed Pullman type crew seats are fast becoming an operating symbol of the technological advances continually being made by American railroads. On some roads the crummies are equipped with the last word in high-speed trucks with roller bearings, beautyrest mattresses on the bunks, individual lockers for members of the train crew, an enamel wash sink, and Butane stove for all the cooking. All the fine comforts of home—or more.

ERIE No. C300—Modern bay window caboose with full radio equipment and high speed trucks now carries the Erie-Lackawanna banner.—ERIE-LACKAWANNA PHOTO

DENVER & RIO GRANDE WESTERN No. 01404—Black way car with four-paned windows in its cupola and white steps for night safety.—G. M. BEST

Latin American Cabooses

The cumulative disaster of modernization and delusions of progress, which have high-pressured American railroads into the purchase of hundreds of millions of dollars' worth of new rolling stock, has not found its way too far south of the Rio Grande. Latin American cabooses are functioning simulacrums of the high iron of the U.S.A. some 50 years ago. There are many exceptions such as the all-steel cabooses riding the rails of the National of Mexico. These crummies for main line service are equipped with the last word in high speed trucks and all-steel construction. On branch lines there still exist cabooses with wooden underframes which, when a pusher is used, require the engine be cut in between the hack and the last revenue car with a steel frame.

INTERNATIONAL RYS. OF CENTRAL AMERICA G332—Homemade narrow gauge caboose as erected by the San Salvador shops some years ago.—G. M. BEST

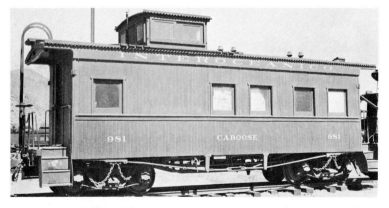

FERROCARRIL INTEROCEANICO No. 981 — Tin roofed slim gauge caboose styled like a typical Mexican short coach.—G. M. BEST

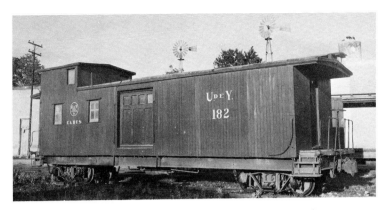

UNITED RAILWAYS OF YUCATAN No. 182—Three-foot gauge *cabus* with one of the most unusual cupola arrangements in Mexico.
—G. M. BEST

COAHUILA & ZACATECAS No. 152—Narrow gauge boxcar like caboose with a large center door, postal mail slot and offset cupola.
—G. M. BEST COLLECTION

PACIFIC RAILWAY No. 3003—Caboose for train crew is coupled to Costa Rica's wooden funeral car at the Puntarenas station.—
B. THOMAS WALSH

Acknowledgments

After waiting many years in vain for someone to write a book telling the story of the caboose, I decided to write one myself, with help from Freeman Hubbard, the editor of *Railroad Magazine*, and here it is. I cannot list all the sources of material that we used in this volume, but we are grateful to them all: oldtime railroad men, rail labor organizations, public relations men of railroad companies, railroad employee's magazines, *Railroad Magazine*, etc. We are in debt to the following for picture material contributed to this book: Richard J. Cook, Everett L. DeGolyer, Jr., Donald Duke, Guy Dunscomb, Mike Eagleson, Henry R. Griffiths, Richard Kindig, Stan Kistler, John Krause, Wm. D. Middleton, Jim Shaughnessy, Dick Steinheimer, and the many others. The author wishes to extend a note of special thanks to Gerald M. Best and Dr. Phil Hastings who contributed the greater portion of the illustrations. Their cheerful contribution to our book is appreciated more than these fine railroad photographers will ever know. We welcome comments, corrections, and additions to this book, the first one of its kind in the history of railroads.

WILLIAM F. KNAPKE
3831 East Flower Avenue
Tucson, Arizona 85716

Index